A Moment Alone with God

Elizabeth Dyer

ISBN-13: 978-1-952308-00-0

Front cover image by Elizabeth Dyer.
Book design by Elizabeth Dyer.
First printed edition 2021.

Positive Publishing Company
38 Merchants Walk, Unit C
Blairsville, GA 30512
www.PositivePublishingCompany.com

www.ElizabethDyer.Me

DEDICATION

I would like to dedicate this book to Charlie Herendon, my father, who finally accepted Jesus as his Lord and Savior just days before his death. Dad, you were my hero and I wish you were here now. I know I will see you again one day.

Also, to Miss Ruby, a dear friend and sister in Christ. She set a godly example of how a woman should live. May you rest in peace, sweet friend.

And Caleb Kinnersley. Many people miss you and loved you so much during your brief time here. May you enjoy the sunny beaches and perfect ski slopes in Heaven.

All three lost their battle to cancer before their families wanted to say goodbye. Their pain ended but heartache remains for those who miss them. I will see you all on the shores of Heaven one day.

CONTENTS

Acknowledgments i

Pop, Goes Me… 1

The Battle Within 7

Celebration and Sorrow 25

Symptoms, Schmyptoms 37

Asking for Help 49

Faith Becomes Sight 63

May Flowers 77

Mark Your Calendars 89

Not So Free 101

The CAT 115

Bad News Phone Call 127

Brain Tumors Can Be Fun 135

Who Needs Privacy Anyway? 149

Asking for Prayer 161

Psalm 34 173

Looking Backward and Forward 183

MRI—My Really Important Moment 191

Confirmation 209

Epilogue: Joy & Guilt 215

God's Plan of Salvation 225

Photo Album 229

ACKNOWLEDGMENTS

Nothing worth accomplishing ever happens alone. I want to thank my friends and family who pushed and encouraged me to get this done. I never thought of myself as an author until the Creative for Christ Writer's Group started meeting in my newest business, a smoothie bar and health food store, now called S&S Smoothies and Supplements.

My family is the reason I have a story to tell. They give me purpose when I get up every day and work to keep things going. They bring me joy. For the times they handled tasks around the house and allowed me to put this story to paper, I am eternally grateful.

Melissa Ray, you are my biggest fan and cheerleader. You encourage me to do more and be more than I ever imagined. You are the best of the best, and I am thankful to call you friend.

Rebecca Collins, your dedication to getting books done helped keep me focused.

Irma Flanagan, grammar specialist extraordinaire, you helped me "dot every i and cross every t" along the way, but even more important, your friendship has helped me get through tough times and grow as a Christian.

I would be remiss if I did not give thanks to Barbara Harkins of Georgia Mountain Publishing. She helped me grow as a writer and forced me to stretch my wings so I could fly.

Thank you to Reverend Todd Flanagan, who helped write the final section of the book—one of the most important parts—and his beautiful wife, Rebecca, who is a wonderful friend and faithful woman of God. Thank you both for all you do to further the Kingdom.

Thank you all from the bottom of my heart. May God bless you all the days of your life. To God be the glory.

POP, GOES ME…

*They prevented me in the day of my **calamity**: but the Lord was my stay.*
2 Samuel 22:19 KJV

I heard the blood-curdling scream—like the ones portrayed in movies—and it happened as I also perceived a loud "pop" of a sound from between my ears. I thought a bomb had gone off in my head.

The pain brought my plump and pregnant body to the floor of my office. I do not know how, but I dragged myself across the varnished wood to the other side of the room and into my favorite comfy beige chair covered with all sorts of pillows. However, it provided no comfort.

The scream reached Robert all the way to his workshop several yards from our house, and he dashed up the hill in North Georgia where we lived on an icy February morning in 2009.

Breathing hard, he asked, "Are you okay? Is the *baby* okay? You're not in labor, are you? I mean, you're not even half-way there."

He ran his still dirty hands soaked with a blend of grease, oil, and other two-cycle equipment fluid through the remains of his hair. His eyes were wide with panic.

When he finally quit blabbering, seeing a single finger raised to my mouth, he realized I had pulled the beige and green pillow to cover my head, and my hands were tight over my ears. I fought to block all sound and light and push myself into darkness.

"Tylenol," I finally whispered as I attempted to answer his questions and move my head as little as possible.

God, PLEASE make this pain go away or just let me die now. I can't take this.

While I remained in the fetal position in the beige chair for the remainder of the day, Robert fed, bathed, and put our five children to bed without me. He kept our rambunctious crew of little ones ages eleven months to eight years out of my office and tried to keep them as quiet as possible.

I caught only a few of the words echoing from the other rooms. I could not fully understand all the conversations, only the occasional higher pitched sounds of conflict as the pain pierced my head like a knife.

"Stop it!" screamed Savannah. Our oldest girl who was six.

"That's mine," Samantha, the middle girl, stated, no doubt yanking her favorite doll from Sharon's hands. This scenario played out daily as they wanted to play with the same object of amusement at the same time. After all, something becomes interesting only when someone else finds it interesting first.

"I'm telling Mommy," Sharon threatened. She was the youngest, smallest, and when angry, feistiest of the three girls. A typical response I also witnessed every day as the toy wars ensued.

Matthew whined for food and John, our oldest child, jumped into action. "I'll feed him, Dad," John said.

I am certain John welcomed the addition of a brother after dealing with three sisters and being the only boy for so long. As a result, John and Matthew formed an incredible bond I hoped would soon include my sixth child—Mark. The brothers also shared March birthdays only two days apart, giving them another reason to be close to each other. John made a great big brother.

Relieved the bits of conversation I understood were nothing unusual, my muscles relaxed a little. Robert seemed to have things under control—as much as possible with five kids, anyway.

Robert had suffered from migraines off and on over the years, and he thought a sudden one had debilitated me. While I recuperated, he took charge of the household and children. The children must have sensed something amiss since I did not tuck them in and kiss them goodnight.

Looking back, I probably should have gone straight to the hospital. However, I would not go through those doors until time for the delivery. Some things still have not changed. I dislike doctors' offices, hospitals, or medicines. On the other hand, the level of pain caused me to make one exception—on the medicine rule at least.

For the next twenty-four plus hours, my beige

chair also became my bed. I hid under a fluffy blanket with lights off and blinds drawn to keep out all light.

I sustained myself on an alternating combination of acetaminophen and ibuprofen. Because of the baby, I had to be careful and not take more than the maximum safe amount. My babies and their health were always more important to me than my own.

The following day, I made it to the bathroom. I stood looking in the mirror. I could find beauty in everyone else. I loved everyone else with all that I had within me, but I had no love left for myself. I looked for the good in people and showed them grace and mercy, giving them understanding for their circumstances.

But as I stood there looking at myself, I thought, *How can anyone love you? Why did you gain so much weight? You look awful like this. You have certainly let yourself go. Is your life **really** worth anything? No one actually loves you.*

I loved God. I adored my family. I admired my friends, and I tried to respect every stranger out there. I just could not understand why God loved me. I knew He sent His son to die for my sins. I became saved when still a young girl.

I clung to the promise of eternal life, but something blocked me from seeing myself as God saw me. Some shadow—a darkness within my mind blocking out the light and any love I should have had for myself—stood in the way.

My negative self-talk finally stopped, and I realized my headache subsided slightly as I felt the urge to blow my nose. A bright red mass kept coming out in chunks until the tissue I held contained a golf-ball sized blood clot. Disgusted but relieved, I believed this ordeal had ended: finished, vanished, completed, done, fading into a dreadful memory.

I was wrong. Dead wrong. This battle signaled the start of a long and difficult war.

THE BATTLE WITHIN

*For thou hast girded me with strength unto the battle: thou
hast subdued under me those that rose up against me.*
Psalm 18:39

During the next several weeks, the headaches
continued. Sharp pains pierced my head at various
locations like a sword. These were not as extreme as
the one on that awful February morning, but they
were not the usual dull throbs of a "regular"
headache.

The loud pop inside my head merely marked the
start of the war—a warning signal of sorts like the
siren sound prompting everyone to take cover and
prepare because things were about to get interesting.
The time to either pick up the sword to fight or flee
for one's life had arrived. Unfortunately, I proved
incapable of doing either.

As in every war, two sides pit themselves against
each other. I, the only civilian witnessing the

atrocities inflicted, but, as time would prove, I was not the only victim.

Two mighty warriors—the Black Warrior and the Red Warrior—dominated my battles. I have no clue what they were fighting for, nor why they chose the inside of my head as the place to compete. Yet, there I was: my body, the battleground, while I remained helpless to do anything about it.

The Red Warrior—the King of Pain and Forgetfulness—took pride in stabbing the interior of my brain with super-sharp, double-edged swords. He wore thick armor, and he sharpened his swords daily. Like a knight, he fought to take over land from heathens that needed eliminating.

At least, that is what I perceived when those searing pains sent me to my knees as if being forced to kneel before his might. Luckily, they did not last long, at least not yet, but they were excruciating.

It did not take me long to learn to go to the floor quickly and voluntarily wherever I stood. This act proved better than waiting for the pain to force me to my knees, bowing to the knight's will. Being forced down only added additional injury to my overweight and pregnant body with bruised knees and an aching back.

The pains increased in intensity and frequency as the days and weeks passed. I had to live through them, as many of us do, before I realized the severity of the situation and before the pain overruled my stubbornness. I could not fathom the root cause of my pain or the extent of the damage the war caused.

I ignored them by keeping my focus on my children and my work. My little ones needed their mom, and I needed them. I realized I would forgo any treatment because of potential harm to the baby growing inside me regardless of how severe the issue. As long as I managed not to scare the kids, I would remain at home and away from the hospital.

I worked only during periods of complete clarity. I took the quality of my work seriously. I have always wanted only the best for my clients. With these periods of clarity becoming less and less frequent, I fell further and further behind on the jobs I needed to complete. Making less and less money to help Robert keep our family well fed and cared for. The lack of steady income marked the start of our financial downfall as the bills came in faster than the paychecks, and credit cards seemed the only solution.

On the other side of the war, the Black Warrior's cruelty came in other forms. He enjoyed surprise attacks against me all the time. He used guerilla warfare and tactics to confuse me as if I had become one of his enemies.

He adorned no unform. Instead, he wore the skins from dead animals tacked together and covered the rest of his body in black filth so that he could hide in the shadows. On his head, he wore the skull and horns of some animal he had killed. I perceived he had to be the heathen the Red Warrior wanted to eliminate, but they injured me instead of each other.

The Black Warrior's favorite form of torture was to change the placement of doorways. Somehow, he magically made them move when I walked through as if he had them on a rope attached through some unseen realm. He booby trapped my entire house with his hidden weapons of warfare.

I would walk along, minding my own business, doing a common thing like going from one room to another—typically my office to the bathroom, as pregnancy often leads to frequent trips. Then, I would have to make a special stop along the way that most people do not. My face frequently smacked the wall, and not a single hit I endured seemed gentle.

They were those squash-your-nose, burst-your-lip, make-your-glasses-one-with-your-face type of smacks. The Black Warrior, tops at trickery and deceit, enjoyed my pain and humiliation. He hid in the shadows laughing at the bruises he had left me covered in.

I did not like these stops in the short distance from room to room, and I involuntarily started a couple of new fashion trends. One of them made black and blue famous since I wore those colors so often and, more to the point, they seemed to be the new colors of my skin. In about a week, a brown and ugly greenish color added to the mix as old bruises started to heal. However, the cycle of colors kept going through the addition of fresh ones.

The second fashion statement became the crazy lopsided look. My glasses did not fair too well in these battles involving the stops at the wall either. The right side of my glasses looked slightly lower than the left, and the difference became more pronounced with each hit to my face.

The eye-care professional I visited said, "Elizabeth, if we adjust these glasses too many more times, they are going to break." She sighed as she gently handed the glasses back to me.

"I know," I replied, "but I cannot afford new glasses right now." I still struggled to keep up with my workload, and my entire family paid the price. I could not justify spending money on anything but the absolute bare necessities.

My glasses, too far gone to ever return to their regular shape, stared back at me from the mirror. As I left the optometrist's office, I held the door for another patient coming in, and she stared at me with wide eyes as she noticed the glasses I wore. Without a doubt, those spectacles were making a spectacle of me wherever I ventured out. The Black Warrior loved my loss of confidence—the miniscule amount I had—as humiliation became a steady state of being for me.

To fight this Warrior, the King of Deceit and Humiliation, I learned to walk more slowly. I also started holding my hand in front of me to catch the wall first. This practice helped tremendously—for a while.

Soon the Black Warrior caught onto my new tactic and threw something else at me. With fewer walls smacking me in the face, he decided to up the ante. He gave me two left feet or two right feet, or maybe he tied my shoestrings together when I was not looking.

Either way, it ended with the same result. Whichever he chose for the moment, my face consequently found something new to hit—the floor or even the ground. Yes, more and more frequently, I found the taste of dirt or Pine-Sol in my mouth and fresh bruises to keep the fashion trend going.

I also hurt my back as I twisted mid-air to keep the brunt of the fall away from my abdomen and growing baby. I had to protect Mark no matter how much it hurt me.

This prayer became a common one during that time:

God, please don't let me hurt my baby when I fall. You showed me him as a promise years ago and I am clinging to the promise. Just give me the strength to protect him against these attacks.

With each fall also came more humiliation. It is hard for others not to laugh when someone falls. Just watch *America's Funniest Home Videos* or a similar show. You likely will view numerous clips of people taking a tumble—some rolling down ski slopes, others missing the trampoline, and more tumbling all over each other attempting some stunt.

However, being the one getting hurt is not nearly as amusing. More than once, I heard cutting remarks about my coordination or lack of grace when I ventured out in public. Sometimes the remarks even came from my own children.

I became the recipient of weird looks wherever I went: the grocery store, department stores, and even church. I saw the same expression on the faces of friends and strangers and heard whispers behind my back.

"What is wrong with her?"

"Do you think she is being abused?"

"What is going on with Elizabeth? She looks terrible."

I hated the person I was becoming more and more. I would say to myself, *now, not only do I look stupid and fat, but I looked beaten up as well. No wonder people make fun of me. Why does everyone have to believe anyone overweight is simply lazy? Can't they also tell I'm pregnant? They have no idea what all I do and how much more I did not so long ago.*

Too independent to seem so helpless and so useless, I struggled to find meaning in my life. The only thing I had felt confident about before any of this began had been my ability to get things done, no matter the circumstances. Now, these warriors stripped my independence away one layer at a time. They seemed determined to plunder all of me and take everything that made me, the person I was, leaving only an empty shell.

My children, of course, did not understand these events. Why would Momma fall? To them, only babies fall when they are learning to walk, and, to them, I was steadfast, coordinated Mom, far from being a baby. I understood the mechanics of walking—running even as I had done so many times with them at the playgrounds. Moms are not the ones needing help to get around the house.

Their young minds were not ready for my reality, so I shared nothing of what I was experiencing. I did not want to scare them. They did not have knowledge of my headaches, the blood clot, or my constant self-deprecating thoughts.

I had watched my father die of cancer, and I vividly remembered the sadness and worry, the prayers and the tears, and the love with the loss. I did not want my children to carry this burden. Therefore, I carried it alone or at least I tried to shoulder it all as the days slowly passed while waiting almost five more months on our newest arrival, Mark.

I even kept much of my experiences away from Robert. I needed him to stay focused on his work and help earn extra money to make up for my lack of ability to do so at the moment.

On one of those "clumsy" days, the children, Robert, and I worked in the yard. We enjoyed the first spring-like day in the North Georgia mountains at the beginning of March. It gave us a chance to leave the confines of the house to enjoy a cool, but comfortable, Saturday outside in the South.

I went to take a step up a wide, but short incline into our storage shed, but my legs would not stay under me. I stumbled, slid down the edge of the incline, and fell off, landing on the ground and receiving a long gash down my leg in the process. Somehow the Black Warrior had left a nail sticking up on the incline, long enough and in precisely the right place for my falling body to find. However, I had managed to protect my belly during the fall and landed on my back instead. The side of my head hitting on a rock.

This gash served as an unwanted reminder. My personal war continued, and I seemed to be on the losing side. My bloody and bruised leg throbbed. Plus, I had hurt my hands while trying to catch my fall. All my efforts, of course, had not kept me from smacking my face on the muddy, wooden incline in the process before tumbling over onto the rock.

The fall confused my four-year-old middle daughter, Samantha. Why would her mom fall so quickly? She ran up the incline and back down, stating, "There is no reason to fall. Just watch me."

She explained further how I should have walked up the incline to avoid falling and demonstrated how easy the task should have been. "See, Mom, just walk like me," she stated matter-of-factly.

She danced and pranced around, not stumbling in the least. Her long dark hair whirled around her face as her hazel eyes sparkled with joy and laughter.

I tried holding myself together and shrugged as if I were okay, which had become my usual procedure, but this time I hurt too much. The Black Warrior mocked me in front of my kids, and I lost my ability to hide the pain. The tears broke through the dam and rolled down my face like a waterfall. My shoulders shook from the force. Robert, with some effort, helped me maneuver my way from the ground into a nearby chair as I assessed the damage this battle had done.

"Look, you made Momma cry," John yelled at Samantha, always protective of me.

"Yeah. Don't cry, Mommy," Savannah replied, with sympathy in her voice.

"I'm okay. My knees and back hurt, and you all understand how you sometimes cry when you get hurt," I said. I attempted to reassure them as I put up a hand, signaling them to stop worrying and no longer bicker. I loved my children, and I wanted to hide my pain from their sight. The blood oozing down my leg and the bruises already popping up all over my legs were showing, however.

"Everything is fine," I announced to all of them.

I hugged Samantha to comfort her as her siblings' remarks had her crying as well. "I know you meant no harm," I whispered in her ear. "Your brothers and sisters don't either. They believe they are protecting their momma. Now, back to playing you go." No more work got accomplished that day.

That day, the Black Warrior won, and I lost—big time. That day, my children noticed.

The incident should have been enough, but the Red Warrior, not willing to concede to his opponent, began attacking with a new strategy as well. The Warrior now loved to sever the lines connecting my brain to my mouth. He decided this game was tops. He created the rules and only he comprehended them. I remained helpless to counterattack until I understood his strategy.

The Red Warrior's attacks occurred while I spoke on the phone with clients. Thankfully, the clients could not witness the ordeal. I would be talking away, explaining a web design feature or new marketing strategy when suddenly halfway through a sentence, I would forget who I was speaking with or why. I would simply go silent, lost in confusion—my mind blank.

The first time this happened, I said, "... I completed the updates you requested. I also added an additional layer of security to prevent hackers from accessing your data." I had a cheery voice and felt relieved to have completed the upgrade to the website.

"The changes look great. I especially like the updated appearance and additional search feature you added," Emily, a long-term client, replied. "Did you have time to complete the text changes I emailed?" she questioned.

I became silent. Unable to complete a thought and answer her, I stared blankly at the phone in my hand. When I moved the receiver back to my ear, I realized I could not hear a dial tone. "Hello?" I asked more than stated ready to hang up the line.

"Hello," Emily said. "I don't know what happened. We seemed to have lost each other. I asked if you had completed the last text changes I sent."

"Oh, yes," I stated quickly, realizing with whom I spoke and coming back into this world from the vale of darkness that had draped over my mind. "The changes are complete. Contact me if you have any more changes once you review everything," I replied, taking some time to remember the first part of our conversation.

"Well, great. Thank you," Emily said. "I will review them shortly and get back with you. I don't know what just happened, but maybe you should get your phone lines checked."

Of course, my phone lines did not cause the problem—or did they? I had experienced problems with the Internet during the last few months. However, my confusion kept me from knowing for certain about anything that had taken place during my conversion with Emily.

"Yes, I might have to call them," I replied as we were hanging up.

I cannot be certain just how long these moments lasted or how foolish I may have seemed. However, several clients did tell me I needed a new phone or to have my phone line checked, and the client's voice would help bring me back. I would usually recognize it and doing so would help me connect the dots and repair those severed mental lines. I also learned to counteract these tactics by making a note about the caller and the purpose of the conversation.

Rosemary—new email addresses

Roger—Change out pictures on home page

William—Add extra items to online store

If I could remember what the discussion and

work entailed, I stood a chance of shortening the periods of silence. I became determined not to let these villainous warriors defeat me or harm my baby. I still had fight in me yet.

God's grace and mercy had these instances occur over the phone. Not being face-to-face required less explaining. After all, I had no reasonable explanation to give and no desire to share my experiences. I tried to keep my personal life private. I simply let the caller keep believing the phone had merely lost its signal because I had no other explanation.

In fact, I did not understand the reasons behind everything that happened. I knew I needed a truce in the war and a peace treaty to follow—a permanent peace treaty. The King of Pain and Forgetfulness in red versus the King of Deceit and Humiliation in black needed to find a new battleground, one not involving me. Otherwise, I would be the loser in this ongoing war. My life, as I knew it, would be demolished like the ruins of a once beautiful city left with only debris after countless air raids. How could I call for a truce?

And if calling a truce proved impossible, were there any more strategies I could use to win? A walking stick? Calling my clients first to make sure my mind started clear? Teaching the kids to do more of the minor chores?

I had to remain on the winning side at least until Mark's birth. My life would then matter less. I had to fight this battle and every battle in the upcoming months for his sake.

Elizabeth Dyer

CELEBRATION AND SORROW

A time to weep, and a time to laugh;
a time to mourn, and a time to dance
Ecclesiastes 3:4

The rest of March brought with it both grief and celebrations. During this time, the hospital admitted Granny Irene, Robert's maternal grandmother and only living grandparent, with kidney issues. She had reached the age of 86 and had been in good health most of her life.

Our daughter Savannah bonded with her on her last visit when Vietta Mae, Robert's mom, brought her to our house. Savannah loved showing Granny her "Matthew Doll" as she had named it in anticipation of her brother Matthew's arrival.

Granny Irene was short and stocky, but she always seemed solid and strong. We found it difficult to imagine her in a hospital bed and even harder to witness. Watching a loved one go from a place of strength to utter weakness and frailty is heartbreaking.

In recent times, Granny Irene had been living with various family members for a month or more at a time. Therefore, we would either see a lot of her or only a little, depending on which relative she lived with and in which town they were residing.

Granny Irene had loved to garden. My favorite memories of her from a few years earlier when she lived alone at Branan Lodge in Blairsville involved her giving us a tour when we visited. She loved to show off all the beautiful blooms, a rainbow of colors dotted amongst shades of green.

"Those are my irises over there," Granny pointed. "And these are my dahlias. The hostas are over there in the shade."

She kept naming off plenty more I couldn't remember and telling us where she got each one. She always remembered who gave her gifts. Her flowers looked beautiful and vibrantly healthy and alive. My own flowerbeds stood in stark contrast, usually filled with dead or dying sprigs. Her skill never ceased to impress me.

Savannah had gotten to visit Granny in the hospital on the tenth of the month, but we did not all go to see her at one time after one family member became very vocal about it. She insisted all the children would be too much trouble in a small confined room. I did not agree, but I also did not argue.

Family feuds have no place during times of sickness or death. I had witnessed enough of them in my childhood to realize a family torn apart during such a crisis might never mend. I did not want to be the cause of the tear.

Therefore, I kept my peace and let their argument go unchallenged. We planned to visit with all our children the next week. Robert and I had a routine down pat. One of us took the children to one activity while the other minded the rest of the crew. After all, we had plenty of practice. We had often scheduled doctor visits and other appointments all on one day to prevent multiple interruptions in our lives.

Two days later, on the twelfth, our son John's birthday arrived. Grandma Vietta Mae called and sang Happy Birthday as usual and we gave him extra attention on his special day. However, he agreed to wait until Matthew's birthday on Saturday, the March 14th, to celebrate with a combined party. He knew his dad and I would be distracted by work during the weekday and he wanted all of our attention on them. In the past, I had done large extravagant joint parties with all the extended family members around plus a lot of people from church.

However, this year the celebration consisted of just us. My health could not hold up to the planning, stress, or entertaining required for such events at this time. I also did not need the additional financial burden or to hear any more remarks about my current state. I wanted to make a wonderful and joyous memory with my kids instead. They meant the most to me, after all.

The Red and Black Warriors were severe enough to deal with daily, not to mention the usual discomfort of pregnancy when one has almost reached the five-month mark. I also realized our family needed to have some extra time together, before our family dynamic changed yet again with our newest addition. Now understanding it might change forever without me if I didn't survive the strain of the impending delivery a few months later.

I kept thoughts of my demise from Robert and even tried to keep them from my conscious mind to no avail.

Mark is the fulfillment of God's promise of the family He revealed to you years ago. Does God really need you around anymore after that? The negative thoughts never seemed to stop.

Matthew's turning a year old did not seem possible, as time went by much too fast. My now chunky little man with dirty blonde hair and bright eyes enjoyed the extra attention. He stuffed his face with chocolate cake, not realizing the significance of a birthday. Our "little" big boy saw cake as a treat either way.

We were in the middle of singing "Happy Birthday" to both of our boys when Robert's phone rang. He ignored the call as we finished off key and out of sync with the joyous chant heard only on such special occasions.

The caller ID revealed Robert's mom, Vietta Mae. Assuming she called to wish Matthew a happy birthday, Robert called her back.

"Hello," she answered.

"Hey. Do you want to sing 'Happy Birthday' to Matthew?" Robert asked.

"Oh, is it his birthday? With everything going on, I'd forgotten it was today. Yes, let me sing 'Happy Birthday' to him," she stated.

Robert held his cell phone to Matthew's ear, and the one-year-old grinned as he listened to his Grandma on the phone. Once he ran off, Robert continued his conversation.

We could not catch the rest of what was spoken, but the look on Robert's face fell from joy to sorrow.

"Okay. Thanks for letting us know," Robert replied as he walked back to my office.

I occupied the kids with sorting the presents for John and Matthew, plus a token gift for the girls, as I slipped into the office to check on Robert. I had made sacrifices and given up money saved for my new glasses to make sure they had a wonderful memory of today. After all, the dead do not need glasses and I knew I could only survive so much of the torture I continued to experience. I sensed more and more the end drew near for me.

"What's going on?" I asked, watching the

expression on his face.

"Granny Irene just died," he said with sorrow in his voice.

I wrapped my arms tightly around him as we stood there for a moment.

Robert finally broke the silence as he stepped back and looked at me, trying to smile. "I remember being a little kid and staying with her. She fixed all of us Kraft Macaroni and Cheese. I absolutely loved it. I didn't get that at home, so it was a special dish to me then. She wasn't the typical granny who cooked everything from scratch, but she made us all feel loved with everything she did," Robert reminisced.

"That sounds wonderful," I replied as I looked at him. After a moment, I stated, "Let's wait until tomorrow to tell the kids. There's no need to ruin their celebration today. There are not enough days to celebrate, anyway."

Robert agreed, and we finished the day with lighthearted laughs and joy at the celebration of life while the sorrow of loss lingered in our hearts.

John received several new toys, but none made him smile as much as his new airplane. Since Robert had taught him about warbirds from his infancy and John had not lost interest, a plane presented itself as the perfect gift for this now nine-year-old.

On the other hand, the sound of ripping paper thrilled Matthew more than the present within. To this young man, the noises it made, and the act of sheer destruction being cheered upon were more interesting than the toys hid within the boxes.

The next morning, we broke the news about Granny Irene's death to the kids. Savannah took it the hardest, as we had expected. We struggled to get through the loss of a loved one. I explained the hope of life everlasting to my small children as we comforted each other through the pain during the next few days.

I knew God from a young age, and I wanted my children to see the same truth and have the same hope in their hearts and minds. Church had been an important part of our lives for years. However, lately, we had missed several Sundays as I lacked the energy necessary for the tasks of dressing, feeding, and getting five children to the vehicle on time. We were also missing the Wednesday night Kids' Stuff program.

"We will always miss Granny Irene, "I told my children as we huddled together. "She was special to all of us, but we need to remember she is now with Jesus. For God promises eternal life to everyone who calls upon the name of Jesus as their Lord and Savior. Isn't that amazing? Can't you just imagine all the flowers Granny will get to tend to now? I bet there are flowers we have never even seen before," I continued.

"Maybe even new colors," Savannah said. "That would be really neat!"

"Yes, and what about dinosaurs? Will they be in Heaven?" John questioned.

"Oh, I bet Granny will be the head gardener up there!" Samantha chimed in.

"What do you think, Sharon," I asked. "Will Granny have a beautiful garden waiting on all of us to visit?"

She answered with a nod and a grin, no doubt thinking about Granny's beautiful flowers and imagining new ones not seen on Earth.

On March 17, we gathered together at Old Liberty Church to bury Granny Irene. Mountain

View Funeral Home presented Granny to her family and friends in a beautiful white casket surrounded by tons of bright-colored flowers. She looked at peace, which helped comfort us all. Much of her family attended and loved on each other through the pain.

After the service, we shared a meal along with stories about Granny.

"Boy, she would've loved all these flowers," Vietta Mae said. "Did you see how beautiful those lilies were?"

"They were gorgeous," I agreed.

"There are so many flowers. They will not all fit on her grave. Her kids will have to take some home and tend to them," she said with a tinge of sadness in her voice. "We can remember her every time we see them."

"Yes, wonderful memories of Granny Irene's flowers," I said with a comforting smile and an arm wrapped around her shoulder.

I found myself wondering what people would say about me when I passed. I hoped I left them with fond memories. I wondered if they would be doing this for me in just a few months.

We celebrated the life she had lived, the children she had birthed and reared, the grandchildren and great-grandchildren, the love shared in the family, her flowerbeds, and all of her unique ways that made her Granny Irene. She would have approved of all the beauty and love surrounding her.

Although we experienced sorrow for our loss, joy remained. Knowing both what Granny Irene gained as she stepped into eternity and feeling thankful for the life her remaining family shared here and now brought us comfort.

Elizabeth Dyer

SYMPTOMS, SCHMYPTOMS

But his flesh upon him shall have pain,
and his soul within him shall mourn.
Job 14:22

Even as a child, I did not complain about pain. I am not sure why maybe because of my mother's insensitivity to whining. As I understood it, sharing feelings of pain equaled a form of whining.

If I fell, her response was, "Get up. Brush it off."

If I cried, she would say, "Now stop that. We will have none of that."

I tried to remain as quiet as possible growing up with my mom, especially after my dad died. If I remained quiet enough, no one noticed me. If I gained attention, my mom summoned me to hear a complaint about a subpar job I completed on a task. I often found myself in trouble for some infraction for which I was not guilty.

If my nieces, who were about my age, came over I would get in trouble for anything they did, even when the grown-ups had knowledge of the real guilty party. I seemed to be the one blamed for all atrocities, however minor they may have been.

On one of the worst occasions I remember, one of my nieces found a heavy stick in our front yard.

"Put the stick down," I instructed, attempting to sound authoritative.

"No!" she screamed at me as she wielded the stick and beat me over the head.

"Ow!" I hollered. "That hurt. Now, give me the stick. It is NOT okay to hurt someone."

She tried to hit me again, but she spotted the grown-ups coming outside. Then, the wailing started. I ended up with a pumpknot and a whooping to go with it. Why? Because she cried first. It did not matter to the adults that I sustained injury—I made her cry. She could do no wrong, and I could do nothing right.

A pattern also emerged with my toys getting

broken every time they came over. Another one of my nieces crammed a stick down my favorite baby doll's mouth. The baby doll no longer cried or drank its milk. Any toys with a pull string no longer worked because they pulled the strings out. Blocks got broken. Arms went missing from dolls. However, my mom instructed me to share and not hide or protect my toys from them.

The interesting part was that they never broke any of their own toys—only mine. My mom never stood up for me, and I never received an apology—from them or their parents—for the harm done.

Now, looking back, I can say at least it kept me reading books and expanding my mind instead of wasting time with broken toys. My favorite way to read kept me hiding outside on every pretty day with a book in hand and finding solitude preferable to the bickering and brokenness.

In addition, a subconscious fear of doctors arose during childhood. My arm swelled redder than a tomato and burned for days when I received vaccines as a child. I saw no benefit to the injury and pain. The viruses and illnesses I did not have and would never get were meaningless to me. The injection caused genuine pain then and the memories linger even now.

Whatever the cause, I trained my mind and my spirit to withstand physical discomfort and keep going sometimes until it was too late. One time, around the age of six, I "gave in" and laid my head in my mother's lap. No one realized I had fought an ear infection for days. Somehow my mind equated the ear infection to a shortcoming on my part. Whimpers escaped from me as the drums beat in my ears. The sound raged, and I remained helpless to make it stop.

The drums beat louder and louder as my whimpers increased in intensity as well until finally—*the explosion*. Hot liquid spurted from my eardrum. The beat of the drums stopped and silenced everything else in the world as well. The fluid oozing down my ear canal meant the infection fought its fight and now the healing began. Eventually, my mother called the doctors, and a round of antibiotics began.

Dozens of rounds on antibiotics and little else to comfort the pain or stop the vicious cycle through the years did not stop the return of ear infection after ear infection. My ear drums ruptured a total of thirteen times before I became a teen. The doctors scheduled surgery to install tubes in my ears.

I also do not know whether we had health insurance during my childhood. I lived in extreme poverty. A visit to a doctor seemed to be a luxury. This, I realize, is another reason I wanted to try to "tough it out" instead of asking for help.

Of course, I can only assume we lacked insurance because we did not discuss such matters. Perhaps not having it is the reason my ears ruptured so many times and became permanently damaged before the doctors took proactive measures.

The surgery to have the tubes installed proved painless and straightforward compared to the previous pain I had experienced. The staff at the hospital remained amiable and not frightening at all. In this instance, I perceived them as providers of a solution and a way to stop my pain.

Although getting used to the unfamiliar feeling in my ears took a while, the drums were now silent and remained so for almost thirty years. That time, doctors, nurses, and the rest of the staff were my friends and my helpers. The ear operation remains the only experience in my youth where I have fond memories of any medical personnel—not because they had done anything wrong, but childhood fears do not have to be rational, after all.

In the spring and summer of 2009, my situation worsened as the days and months passed and I still fought to be tough. The battle continued, and I remained the one on the losing side, but at least all of my checkups showed the baby growing and in good health. I would not bring myself to consider something else could be wrong with me, and I focused on my children and not myself.

I never saw myself worthy of concern. Those feelings of not being good enough were ingrained in me from a young age. I had not let them go. I did not understand how to. Although a horrible man, Hitler had one thing right, "If you tell a big enough lie and tell it frequently enough, it will be believed." I wholeheartedly accepted myself as unworthy.

My work piled up and clients became impatient. Some clients required my attention at their office or home for mobile computer repair services. However, because of the Red Warrior's attacks, I no longer trusted myself to drive. Because of the Black Warrior's increased attacks, I had to ignore almost every call.

At the same time, my husband and I had to feed and clothe our children as well as pay the other bills. A credit card limit would only carry us so far and get us nowhere, adding more stress as debt piled up. So, I tried to earn every dollar possible.

Just over two months after the war in my head first began, I vividly remember the last instance in mid-April, which forced me to confront my symptoms. After this service call, I realized the time had come to talk more in depth about the events to my midwife and trusted medical professional, Miss Sheila.

My ever patient and considerate husband, Robert, had picked up a computer from a long-time client, Sam. The repair took me a few days to complete instead of the typical few hours. With the PC updates complete, my family loaded themselves into our vehicle and Robert drove us to Sam's home.

After we arrived, Robert carried the machine inside. I followed, not trusting myself to lift anything I could not afford to take with me to the ground on one of my frequent falls. Robert returned to the vehicle to stay with our children during the few minutes I needed to connect everything and explain the recent updates to Sam.

I made it into the house and found the correct room. No walls had smacked me yet. I gave myself a mental high five. Perhaps, I would make it through this repair visit.

While I started connecting the machine, I even carried on a conversation with Sam, a small thing that seemed normal. He and I discussed the recent software update I had completed, plus how to avoid viruses and stay away from malware. Then, we started talking about family.

Sam, a proud father and grandfather, told me beautiful stories about his son and grandson. His eyes twinkled with delight while he spoke about them. I enjoyed hearing about his family's antics and shenanigans, while I talked about how my kids and family size had grown. Sam had seen my family increase from only John, the oldest, to my youngest, number six, Mark, pushing on my belly with his kicks and somersaults.

He remembered I had homeschooled my older kids for the last couple of years. Sam, a retired schoolteacher, possessed a plethora of schoolbooks. He still kept them around his house. Once, he even gave a few to my oldest son, John, who loved to learn and remained especially fond of Sam.

Sam asked me about my homeschool routine for

the following school year. The public schools had just announced they were starting earlier for the upcoming year. I, on the other hand, began after Labor Day.

"The public school is starting the first week of August this year. Are you planning on sticking to the Monday after Labor Day or changing your schedule to match theirs? Or have you decided?" he asked.

Before I had time to answer, the Red Warrior **attacked**! He hit me with one of his best ambushes yet. I stood there, in Sam's home, staring blankly at a calendar. Paralyzed and confused, my mouth would not move. No words would come. However, my mind kept going, trying to make a new connection, trying to complete a thought. I perceived the information existed in there somewhere, but how could I find it?

"What did he ask?" I thought to myself. "Why am I staring at a picture? ... A month, a day, what was it? ... That's a calendar, right? ... What are those? ... That's a pretty picture ... Letters, I see letters ... I like the ocean ... What are letters for? ... Why was I thinking about months? ... Words, letters make words ... What are the months? Don't I know them? ... Words, you read words. Do I know how to read? … That's a pretty boat … Yes, I know how to read. So why can't I read those letters, no words."

"April," I finally said.

The perplexed look on Sam's face matched the one on mine. "No, that's not right, but I can't remember," I said after another lengthy pause.

"Elizabeth, I forget things sometimes, too, but I'm a lot older. What has happened to you? Are you okay?" he asked with concern.

"I don't know. I suppose I have to see the doctor," I replied as tears glistened in the corner of my eyes.

Thankfully, my husband came to the rescue. He came back inside to find out why the service call was taking so long. It had been over half an hour, and the kids were getting restless waiting for me. Before we left, Robert finished hooking up Sam's computer because, along with everything else, I had forgotten how.

Me, with a bachelor's degree in Information Technology (IT). Me, with years of repair experience. Yes, me! No longer able to perform the simple task of hooking the cables to the back of a computer.

I felt useless, scared, and alone.

I sank down in the passenger seat and stared ahead only with incomplete thoughts running through my mind. I did not want to worry Robert or scare our kids, but, somehow, I seemed to be frightening them anyway. That day, I scared a client, too. Actually, that day's events scared me as well. What happens to someone when their thoughts no longer process and their body no longer functions? Would this be the end of me?

My kids lost their mom, and my husband lost his wife to these ailments that were taking everything I had to offer. I had lost myself, my identity. I did not understand how to get it back.

Was I okay? No, I admitted the answer without a doubt. I just couldn't comprehend why.

Sam made my husband promise to get me to the doctor and soon. I no longer argued. I would not protest. I do not think I would have known how to, anyway. I wanted to raise the white flag of surrender, but my weakened body found it too hard to lift.

Elizabeth Dyer

ASKING FOR HELP

For at that time day by day there came to David to help him, until it was a great host, like the host of God.
I Chronicles 12:22

The following day my husband and I arrived at the office of my midwife, Miss Sheila. Not for a special visit to deal with the pain and discomfort I experienced, but merely for one of my regular healthy baby checkups. We kept an eye on twenty-nine-week-old Mark as he worked to expand the breadth of my already large waistline.

The measurements indicated that Mark was growing at a healthy rate. A monitor also let us hear his fluttering heartbeat.

"There's his little heartbeat," Miss Sheila announced as the monitor finally found the right spot to listen to the squirming little one in my belly. "Around 140 beats per minute. Perfect. Just perfect."

The sound brought a smile to my husband's face

and mine. Although I did not know what he would look like at birth, this little bundle of joy already owned part of my heart.

I sat up and Miss Sheila asked, "So how has Momma been?"

"Fine. Just ready for Mr. Marky's arrival," I said. My mind threw up a stop sign with all of its strength. "Well, not really. I have been having some strange episodes lately."

"Well, tell me about them," she said with a concerned expression.

"I suppose I should have told you much sooner, but I ignored them, and frankly, I just get excited to learn about how Mark is doing when I come here." I recounted all the major events, beginning in February with the pop and ending with a recant of the incident at Sam's house the day before.

I did everything possible to protect Mark, but now I worried that my episodes might have caused him duress. Would they reach him? Could they harm my innocent and tiny baby? Could they make me go into labor too early?

I put my trust in Miss Sheila. I always found her

to be an amazing, intuitive woman of God, filled with wisdom. She consulted others when she did not know the answer, never letting pride get in her way. After I completed my story, to no surprise, she requested the consulting physician, Dr. Breedlove, to come talk with me.

The experiences I described were, judging by the puzzled look on their faces, not a common occurrence. Dr. Breedlove referred me to Dr. Smith, an ear, nose, and throat specialist whom I had seen a few years before. She had removed my tonsils and performed miracles on my allergies with a surgical procedure on my turbinate.

I trusted the opinion of each of these medical specialists completely, which seemed remarkable considering my background with medical personnel. Miss Sheila, after all, had been part of each of my deliveries, with Dr. Breedlove having my full confidence to back her in any situation. Dr. Smith viewed my discomfort and persistent sinus infections as something to be cured rather than part of how my life would be.

"Go to the front desk and they will set up an appointment for you with Dr. Smith," Dr. Breedlove instructed as he handed me a referal.

I handed the lady the paper and as soon as she set some other items to the side, she made the call. "Is this coming Tuesday at 4:15 p.m. okay?" She looked up at me.

"Yes," I said, and Robert agreed.

"Dr. Smith had a cancellation," she said as she hung up the phone. "It must be your lucky day. It is usually a three-month wait."

"Thank you," I said and Robert and I headed back home.

Thank you, God. Perhaps I will get answers soon and the healing can begin. Maybe I can I find myself again.

This opening, less than a week away, made it evident to me God was already at work throughout this ordeal. His plan already in place, I needed to merely live out each part as it fell exactly where He meant it to be.

This beautiful mess I called life transformed into a bigger picture, a puzzle of sorts. Those individual pieces were now forming an actual scene that looked entirely different from any single piece considered alone. Sometimes I wished the box appeared.

Perhaps, a view of the completed scene would reveal a clearer picture of everything I worked to build and assemble.

During the office examination, Dr. Smith used a camera to check every crevice in my head and even the backs of my eye sockets. She failed to discover anything that would have caused the popping noise I heard over two months earlier or anything that would account for the ongoing headaches. She also found the first incident I described as being unusual.

"I've never heard of anyone experiencing anything quite like what you are describing," Dr. Smith stated. "In my exam, I did not see any tumors, and that is a good sign. However, I do see where you are still experiencing some bleeding in your nostrils. I am going to cauterize those areas for you. I am also going to recommend that Dr. Breedlove order a CAT scan to be performed for further investigation."

She completed the procedure, and I left to go about the rest of my day with an atrocious smell in my nostrils—one of burnt flesh, my flesh. On a positive note, I would no longer have a red tissue every time I blew my nose.

Later in the evening, one word kept racing

through my mind: ***Tumor***. My thoughts did not include the possibility of a tumor, yet my dad and a dear friend, Miss Ruby, both entered my thoughts a lot lately. This word brought back memories of their final days.

My dad died of cancer.

I still remember the last time I walked into his hospital room at the tender age of eleven. He raised up in the bed with his white and blue hospital gown draped over his body. I could see his bones everywhere and golf-ball sized knots riddled his body. It looked to me as if he had been beaten with a golf club.

He scarcely looked like the man I called Dad all of these years. He was not even wearing his fedora hat. He had always put his hat on first thing in the morning and took it off late at night. I rarely saw him without his fedora, but here he was not wearing it that day.

I went to jump on the bed to sit beside him, but my mom stopped me and directed me to a nearby chair. I just wanted to be next to my dad but my mom forced me away. I held back tears of rejection and fear. I had to spend much of our time at the hospital simply sitting in the waiting room—alone and not understanding the transformation happening to my dad.

Regardless of how he looked, my dad always put on a smile when around me and never let me know the pain he experienced. He did not complain about his discomfort. He did not curse God for this illness or the unfairness of it all. He simply smiled.

I did not understand the horrid transformation his body underwent as he lost weight and grew knots. Even though I saw it all over him, a misunderstood villain, cancer, remained. I also did not realize this visit would be our final one and my last time to say *"I love you."* I still wish I had been able to have more time with him.

A few days later, I awoke at 4:00 a.m. to the news of my father's death. Until that point in my life, I did not understand loss—absence, yes, but not loss.

There is a permanent hole in my heart. I lacked words to express the pain for which I had not been prepared. I had never experienced this level of grief. The wave of grief simply crashed into me, threatening to drag me out to sea until its grip faltered for a moment only to come back again and start the process over. To this day, I still grieve the loss of my dad and desire a little more time with him.

The year of my father's death became my first experience with this horrible beast, but not my last. That year alone, I lost a total of five family members. The waves of grief were crashing in on me so hard I believed I would drown, and I think part of my mother drowned in the sorrow. Neither of us ever felt the same again.

No one goes through such loss without being transformed. The question is, will we come out being a beautiful butterfly? Will we embrace the knowledge and understanding that life is short and try to make something spectacular in the brief time we have? Or are we going to be defeated and made into something less than we were when we began?

In more recent years, I lost a dear friend—Miss Ruby. Although she was distantly related to my husband, I became acquainted with her when Robert started mowing her lawn. Her husband, Junior, passed away, and she needed help keeping everything maintained.

While Robert tended to the lawn, I visited with Miss Ruby, a wise woman who held solid Christian values. I admired everything about her. She never seemed judgmental of others. When someone did something wrong, she would say, "They ought not to do that." She would also say things such as, "Christians should learn just to get along."

She soon started showing me the sewing machine collection remaining in her garage from the business she and her husband ran.

"You and Robert as a couple remind me of how Junior and I were together. How the two of you work to fix things," Miss Ruby said with a sparkle in her eyes. "Junior and I spent years repairing these old sewing machines and selling them."

"I love the look of the old pedal sewing machines," I said. "What is this one?" I asked, pointing to one I found especially beautiful.

"That one is a White," she replied. "Junior never got around to fixing it before he passed." After a pause, she said, "I have a special one I want to show you."

I followed her back into the house and she ran her hand over a small Singer sewing machine. With tears glistening in her eyes, "This is the last machine he ever fixed for me," she said, her hand still on the singer, which kept them connected even though he no longer lived.

In fact, her eyes sparkled whenever she spoke of Junior, and time stood still as she relived a precious memory. Then, they would start to tear again as she came back to the present, a time she no longer shared with the love of her life.

I understood grief all too well, and our losses became another reason why Miss Ruby and I befriended each other instantly. She kept telling me how Robert and I brought back memories of Junior and her when they were younger.

Her pain left her unable to sleep in the bed she had shared with Junior or to use the beautiful Singer sewing machine he repaired. She felt as if somehow using it might take away the last trace of Junior. The couch became her bed, and the sewing machine sat unused against the wall, a monument to him.

Eventually, she moved to a new home with a new a bed in which she could sleep. I think the change of surroundings brought her some peace and some sadness. With her move, one of her children started taking care of her lawn. Therefore, my visits with her were less frequent and, oh, how I longed to spend more time with her. Just before John's birth, Robert and my awkward pregnant self went out of our way on a trip home to stop and chat with Miss Ruby. She had gotten settled into her new home, but she seemed different—agitated. I never remember seeing her angry in the least before that moment. She also got confused and called Robert by the wrong name. She even forgot I was expecting a boy.

I asked her, "Are you okay?" the same question others would ask me many times almost a decade later.

Only a week or so after our visit, we learned she had a brain tumor. The doctors had given her little chance of survival.

We took our newborn baby, John, to introduce him to Miss Ruby. When we arrived, we found her house crowded with family members. She lay in a hospital bed in her living room. She remained coherent only briefly. Then, she spoke curse words I did not even think she knew as pains ran through her body.

I started to cry. I had seen death enough times to realize when the grim reaper hovered in the shadows.

The speed at which it came to her, one of my favorite people in the world, shocked me. My heart ached at the thought of losing her. I had just found her—a treasure of a friend worth more to me than all the rubies in the world.

A few days later, we laid Miss Ruby to rest.

She and my father had both changed rapidly at the end. Both became agitated and forgetful. Both became confused, almost forgetting me entirely. Both had meant so much to me.

A tumor, or multiple tumors, had taken them from me. I had not considered having one myself as a possibility, not until the word came out of Dr. Smith's mouth. I thought I might be dying, but not from a tumor.

Since Dr. Smith stated she could not see a tumor, why did this word haunt me? Was I changing in the same way Miss Ruby and my father had before the end? I had become forgetful, but was I also agitated? I became angry with myself, so perhaps, without even realizing or remembering it, I had shown anger towards others.

The Black and Red Warriors trapped me behind

the front lines, and I cannot imagine how it looked from the other side. I could not compare what I experienced to what I witnessed in my dad and Miss Ruby. However, these thoughts remained and brought anxiety to add to the stress and pressure I felt over the debilitating experience.

This anxiety, in turn, made it hard for me to pray. I was not sure why, but it seemed to take over my mind. My thoughts could not even turn to God—my only comfort in times of trouble.

The warriors were pushing me further and further into darkness and trying to block me from the light. I had to find a way to pierce their veil of darkness and allow the light to shine on me again.

FAITH BECOMES SIGHT

Now faith is the substance of things hoped for,
the evidence of things not seen.
Hebrews 11:1

During my next checkup with Miss Sheila, she informed me Dr. Smith and Dr. Breedlove consulted on my condition. They agreed to perform a CAT scan after the birth of Mark. So, for the next several weeks, we moved into a pain-management phase.

For the most part, the plan seemed simple. I experienced pain, and I dealt with it. I refused any pain medications with the potential to harm my baby no matter how small the probability. This strategy meant I took only an occasional acetaminophen and dealt with the rest.

I was tough after all, wasn't I? I had to be. I had birthed five children already without an epidural or pain meds. I convinced myself I could handle this challenge. No other choice existed in my mind. My baby's health trumped my own.

Mark needed ten more weeks of growth until his projected arrival date, July 6. Ten weeks or seventy days is not such a long time unless, of course, one is near the end of a pregnancy. Those final days always became miserable for me with a continual backache and frequent trips to the restroom. In addition, I still experienced searing pains in my head at random intervals. Ten weeks seemed much too long.

Only a little over six months earlier, I received news of Mark's upcoming arrival! Yet, I *expected* him for some years. In less than three months, I would be introduced again to this miracle of God.

In the early years of my marriage, a doctor told me I would never carry children of my own. After three years of trying, I resigned myself to becoming a foster parent with the hopes of one day adopting.

However, God had other plans for me. While working on the monstrous stack of paperwork I believed would finally allow children to call me "Mommy," I discovered I already expected a child of my own.

Once John, my blonde-haired and blue-eyed boy

with light skin like his momma, arrived, my life seemed complete, and I did not expect to deliver any more children. In my mind, God allotted one miracle per person, and John's arrival counted as a miracle. After all, miracles are in short supply, are they not?

In addition, a complicated delivery, in which the survival of my first-born and me became uncertain, left me believing and vowing I would never deliver another child.

Yes, I am sure God laughed at my words—an inside joke in Heaven—and I, too, can now laugh. God's plans for my life vastly differed from my own. However, He knows far more than I and His superior plans lead to greater rewards.

Relatives gave us a baby shower before John's arrival, and I received all kinds of items I needed as gifts: crib, car seat, highchair, clothes, and diapers. When John outgrew the infant car seat—in my certainty of having only one child—I soon relieved my household of such an "unneeded" item and sent it on to bless someone else. When he needed a big-boy bed, I gave the crib to someone else. The process continued until none of the infant items remained.

When my son was only a year and a half old, my

husband talked about a baby girl. He would look at baby dresses anytime we approached the infant section in a store. I fought the idea of another pregnancy and delivery.

Shortly thereafter, we were sitting behind a couple with an infant girl at church one Sunday morning while eighteen-month-old John enjoyed frolicking with other children in the nursery. My husband grinned and played with the baby before the service started. Then, he looked at me with a knowing look, and to him all I said was "noooooooooo," with a smile.

Then, lo and behold, what did the preacher, Pastor Brock, speak about only moments later—"As Christians, we all too often say 'no' to God's blessings." Now, I realize the pastor had overheard my words just moments before he walked behind the pulpit. However, he prepared the message long before he spoke to the congregation that day.

I sat in the pew, listening wholeheartedly with an imaginary spotlight shining on me. Yes, God brought me under conviction and in a big way. However, I admit it often takes the proverbial two-by-four over my head for me to catch on. That day, His message, undeniable as the plank of wood, smacked me while sitting in the church pew.

Only a few weeks later, we learned of Savannah's impending arrival. Wait? What? Another baby for Robert and me? I ventured to the store to buy another car seat, crib, and a plethora of other infant items to again fill my home.

Savannah arrived with light brown hair, dark chocolate eyes, and the darker complexion of her dad. In just over a year, she outgrew the infant car seat, and I sent it to a new home to bless a different family. Then, when she got too big for the crib, we found a new home with a baby to sleep on its comfy mattress.

Without a doubt, I would NOT have more children. Here we were with one beautiful baby girl and one handsome little man—the perfect family, or so I thought. One boy and one girl: the American dream family, right? What more could I ask for?

Nonetheless, only a little over sixteen months after Savannah made her appearance, I learned I was expecting *again*. A third miracle? I considered myself unworthy. My roller-coaster emotions and tight budget left me unprepared to start crib shopping again so soon. However, Samantha's impending arrival made getting these items a necessity.

I prayed.

I prayed for God to tell me a number. *"Lord, you know our finances are tight. You know I want to be a good steward of what You have given to us. However, Lord, I made the wrong decision to get rid of things that I now understand I still need. Lord, will you please tell me how many children I am supposed to have.*

Lord, You blessed me and opened my womb. Just as You did for so many women in the Bible and many throughout the years we do not even know about. I will follow Your will, just please guide me and give me a number so I can make wise choices and prepare. In Jesus' name. Amen."

This scripture came to mind from Genesis 30:22, "And God remembered Rachel, and God hearkened to her, and opened her womb."

During the night, God answered my prayer with a vision:

I stood on top of a hill with lush green grass under my feet, in a meadow outlined by a forest. God stood behind me, and although I could not turn and see His face, I felt His presence surround me. First, God showed me two adolescent boys playing close together. He called them Mark and Matthew.

The smallest one had dark brown hair and chocolate-colored eyes that sparkled with mischief. The other had light brown hair sprinkled with hints of gold and a smile that could melt the coldest of hearts. They stopped and stared at me with a grin all over their faces as if they were as curious about me as I felt about them.

When they looked away, my attention drifted down the hill. I saw a young blonde girl not too far from them. She shyly raised her hand and smiled my way. I returned her smile as confusion washed over me.

I did the unthinkable. I stood and argued with God. "God, these are beautiful children, but they can't be mine. I mean, I have John, a boy, as my oldest and then Savannah. The baby I am carrying now is believed to be another girl…."

God swiftly ended my arguments as He often does, this time with a simple movement of His hand. He pointed over my shoulder, and my gaze moved to three other children and my husband. Robert stood off in the distance below all of them, near the tree line.

John, my blue-eyed, blonde-haired boy who stood almost as tall as I am and who looked mature appeared nearest to me. Savannah, with her deep brown eyes, emerged also as an older version of her current self. She stood not too far below John on the hill. Then, at an even greater distance away materialized a girl I could only imagine being Samantha who would be born in a few short months. Long dark brown hair hid her face until she looked up at me and revealed her hazel.

Yes, I had an ineloquent response to God, as all I could say was, "Oh." It was my most humble response as I stood in shock admiring the young ones which He would soon bless me with.

That night, during the dream, God introduced me to all six of my children. He showed me an image of what my family would look like in the years to come. John, Savannah, Samantha, Sharon, Matthew, and Mark were to fill not only my small home but my heart.

This vision left me with feelings I had never experienced before. I had a sense of purpose in my life—a purpose way beyond myself. When I awoke the next morning, I had the desire to share my experience with others.

Robert listened to me intently enough and then met me with an understandable response—one most men receiving unexpected and unprepared-for news would give—a blank stare. This lack of response was not what I hoped it would be. However, I had had no expectations of Robert since he previously went silent for three days when I told him I had a positive pregnancy test for the first time. I just took his reaction for shock and kept moving forward with plans of preparation.

I should have trusted God's gift of vision. However, I questioned what I had seen in the upcoming months because other Christians doubted the validity of my vision. Was it, as they insisted, just an ordinary old dream with no meaning because I slept with children on my mind? Should I have simply kept the news of the vision to myself? Didn't Joseph from the Bible get himself into trouble sharing his vision?

The dream stayed with me until after I gave birth to Samantha. Yet, I still questioned it.

I prayed a second prayer when Samantha reached about a week old, "Lord, if the dream was from You, will You please give me confirmation?"

The next morning, Robert, our three children, and I ventured off to church. On our way into the sanctuary, a lady stopped and asked me, "Is this little one number *six*?"

"No, I have only three children," I replied.

"Don't worry. You will have *six* soon enough," she stated matter-of-factly and turned and walked away.

Her words stuck with me, but I did not accept her prophecy as my confirmation.

At the end of the church service, our pastor introduced my family to Reeda Faye Kelley. She paused for a moment, apologized for being in a hurry, glanced at Samantha. Then, she turned to me and said, "Don't stop until you have *six*." Immediately, she continued her forward trek. Well, her statement stuck with me and had me squirming.

After we left the church, we journeyed to the grocery store for some needed essentials. A lady called my name from several feet away. I did not recognize her, but I stopped and allowed her to catch up as she certainly recognized me. She peeked under the teddy bear blanket covering the infant car seat and my newborn, Samantha, in the buggy.

"So Elizabeth, you have *six* now?" she asked.

"No, I only have three," I replied, once I found my ability to speak again.

"Don't worry. You will have *six* before you know it," she said, as if she possessed some secret knowledge, and walked away.

I gazed toward the heavens and smiled. "Thank you, God, for answering my prayer." I could no longer doubt my vision, a glimpse of the future—my future—my future family.

With the confirmations, I leaped into action. I rearranged my home using every room for a specific purpose. I created a boys' room and a girls' room, each equipped with bunk beds and a trundle bed. I purchased things in sets of six, such as picture frames for the newborn baby pictures. I saved the crib, car seats, and baby clothes, organizing everything as I proceeded. Yes, I prepared a home for six children—three girls and three boys.

I did occasionally share my story when someone came over and asked me why I had six picture frames on the wall. They also questioned the paper with the names Matthew and Mark in the empty ones. However, I never again expected anyone to believe me, and I no longer cared if they thought of me as crazy. Living out God's purpose for my life became my mission.

His vision gave me the strength I needed to withstand the criticism from strangers and friends alike. It gave me the strength to endure pressures from family members. I am sure they had good intentions when insisting that we find a permanent "fix" to our "problem" of having so many children. Yes, God gives us all the strength we need in whatever way He chooses.

Now, all these years later, this vision has become my reality. I had been expecting Mark the longest, for over five years, and I would hold him in my arms in only a few weeks. God, however, had known everything about him from the beginning of time. Therefore, I accepted God had a plan for the war and everything else I experienced. I put my trust in Him as I waited for the ultimate moment when my faith would become my sight. I realized I still had a purpose while I carried Mark.

However, with all the joy of Mark's impending arrival also came the anxiety and questions. Was my purpose in life over once Mark was born? Was I to birth these six wonderful little people only to have no further part in raising them? Uncertainty about whether my body had the ability to withstand the labor remained in my thoughts. I wondered if Mark's beginning marked my end.

MAY FLOWERS

But the fruit of the Spirit is love, joy, peace,
longsuffering, gentleness, goodness, faith...
Galatians 5:22

Robert and John's desire to see airplanes increased continually. Specifically, warbirds. Robert's number-one hobby remained watching and reading about these marvelous machines.

On the 2nd of May, Dobbins Air Force Base in Marietta, Georgia (only two hours from our home) scheduled an airshow. I knew I must find the strength and energy to go, regardless of how I felt.

We would be out in the blistering sun for hours, so I needed to prepare. In the days before, I somehow managed to pack snacks for the hungry, drinks for the thirsty, strollers and diapers for the young ones, sunscreen for the fair-skinned, and extra clothes just in case.

Most importantly, I got the kids ready in the morning. We were off on an adventure, and they could not wait.

Of course, their excitement led them to be restless and ready to get out of the vehicle. Since the airshow was within a reasonable distance from our home the restlessness was short-lived. Therefore, we arrived to the excitement and thrills of airplanes with my sanity still intact.

Once we got there, it took several minutes to get all the necessities out of the vehicle and Matthew into a stroller. Although he could walk, the sizeable crowd discouraged us from letting him move about on his own. I pushed the stroller with our little man, and Robert carried a foldable chair for me to sit in whenever I got tired. I expected the need to be far more frequent than normal even for a woman as pregnant as I was, complete with swollen legs and ankles plus an aching back.

There were miles of asphalt and concrete on which to walk. It may have been early May, but with scarcely a cloud in the sky it seemed more like a hot, humid day in mid-August. The perfect weather to experience an airshow or heat stroke. My health and the humidity indicated a greater likelihood of heat stroke…

"Hey, John, check out the SBD Dauntless. It was a dive bomber during World War II and helped sink four Japanese ships during the battle of Midway. This Dauntless is one of only two in flying condition today," Robert stated as he pointed to one of the warbirds.

"Can we go check it out?" John questioned with curiosity in his eyes and a skip in his step.

"Of course, son. That's why we are here," Robert replied as they walked off. I took a seat and waited, admiring the planes from more of a distance.

At the next section, I heard Robert continuing to educate John.

"Look over there at the Japanese D3A Val Dive Bomber," Robert started.

"Really? Dad, I thought all of those were not in flying condition anymore," John interrupted.

"Correct," Robert said, patting John on the back. "This one is a replica. It was originally a T-6 trainer, but they rebuilt it to disguise it as the Val for the movie *Tora! Tora! Tora!* Do you remember watching the movie with us?"

"Oh yeah. I remember it," John replied. "Wow! It's so cool to see one in person that I saw in a movie…."

The boys did not want to miss anything, but I needed a break about every half-hour. Whenever possible, I would locate the folding chair we brought from home in a central spot within a section of several planes on display. I tried to relax under the shade of a wing while some kids rested their tired feet. All the while Robert, John, and whatever other interested child examined those feats of modern science and vintage craft alike.

Normally, I enjoyed looking over the planes and observing them while they flew. The stunt planes and their acrobats tend to be my favorite. They make me want to soar in the sky and experience the adrenaline rush. I watched one head toward the ground only to do a tight turn just seconds before impact and go right back up for the clouds.

In those days, however, I experienced little to no interest in anything. As I sat in the shade of one of the planes, I realized how I waited on death and how on some level I wanted to die. I got to the point of feeling worthless, making it hard to keep going. Mark and my other children gave me reason to get out of bed each day.

Thankfully, neither the Black Warrior nor the Red Warrior launched an attack on me that day. I tried to hold on tight to those short-lived moments. I juggled enough without their torture.

Later, in the afternoon, we joined the larger crowd to get the best view of the airshow aerial acrobatics.

"Kids, check out that C-17 transport plane. It is one of the Air Force's newest transport planes. It can carry heavy loads and take off in short distances," Robert informed us all. "John, this is the same plane you saw take off at the Robins Air Force Base when you were little. Do you remember it?"

"Oh, yeah! Wasn't that where we went to watch the Blue Angels? I think I remember," John replied.

This show featured the Air Force Thunderbirds. They put on a spectacular airshow that did not disappoint our crew. The flying acrobats got the attention of all our children and held it, or so I believed. For a brief moment, I enjoyed snapping one photo after another with my Canon camera. During a break between shows, I was taking shots of the kids when I realized Matthew had disappeared!

"Robert!" I said with urgency and fear in my voice. "Where's Matthew? Do you have him?"

"No!" He sounded startled and concerned. "He was right between us in the stroller."

Two nearby families started helping us search. We found Matthew a few yards behind us where he had pushed himself. This clever little boy discovered how to wiggle forward until his feet touched the ground, and he joyfully orchestrated his great escape.

Matthew giggled and grinned as we pushed him back to our original spot. He was simply playing a game. I, however, experienced an adrenaline rush, and the Warriors attacked. Debilitated in my chair, the Earth's core seemed to pull me downward trying to consume my remnants. The rest of the airshow continued with no notice from me.

Shortly after the show finished, we started home. My condition forced me to spend the majority of the next few days in bed recovering. I judged myself more worthless now than I had ever been.

We did not take any more family outings in May until the last Sunday. Robert insisted we do something to celebrate Mother's Day even though it had already passed. Therefore, off to the Greenville Zoo we would go, the kids deciding a trip to the zoo would be the perfect way to show their Mom love.

We performed the same routine as before except this time I needed some "insurance". Otherwise, I would not have been able to relax at all. I needed a faster way to find any escape artist this round and decided coordinated shirts would suffice. With all the kids dressed in orange, we headed off on another adventure. I prayed this one would not leave me debilitated and in bed.

Once we arrived, I assigned different hands to Matthew's stroller continually, so someone would have hold of it anytime I needed to let go. Thankfully, this trip happened without any scares.

"Hey, Mom, look at the lion," Savannah said as she ran up to the glass. "Did you see his big teeth when he yawned?"

"Mom, come on, let's look at the giraffes," John pulled on my sleeve. Sharon and her dad were already sitting there staring at these long-necked, gentle creatures.

The kids were getting to and through the animal displays much faster than I was. I called out to Robert. "Hey, honey. Can you take the kids to the playground over there while I rest here and enjoy the animals for a minute? They are running through here faster than I can keep up."

"Of course. You rest a minute. You seem exhausted," Robert answered.

He took the kids to the small playground within the zoo. They enjoyed running at top speed while I caught my breath. My feet were acting as if stuck in concrete every time I moved. I needed to regain my strength to make it through the rest of the day.

Soon, we snaked our way on down the path to the orangutans. Baby Bob, the young ape on the other side of the glass, mesmerized Matthew and fascinated the other kids. He played and had as much fun as they did.

I loved taking pictures and observing the animals. However, seeing the kids have so much fun together became my favorite part of the day. My dedication to them was unwavering.

We finished our tour, taking about three hours longer than usual in order to allow me to keep pace. We let the kids romp in the large playground in the nearby park, allowing me a few more moments to rest. They burned through some of their ever-abundant supply of energy. Oh, if only I had a drop of what they had to get me through that day and every day.

On the drive back, we stopped for a picnic dinner at the South Carolina Botanical Garden at Clemson University. I took more photographs and rested, while the kids enjoyed more playtime. I wanted them to have fond memories of our time together after God called me home.

"La, la, la, la, la," Samantha sang out as she took center stage on the white gazebo.

"It's my turn now," Savannah said as she jumped up the steps.

One kid after another "put on a show" for Robert and me before jumping down and running through the grassy space surrounded by flowers.

During this trip, I fell in love with hostas. Their leaves were big and beautiful. Some were solid green, while others had a bluish tint to them. Still others displayed variegated leaves with stripes of white on the inside or around the edge. Species after species of this hardy plant laced the gardens. That the variety and beauty in their leaves would last for a season, unlike blooms that last only a few days, fascinated me.

We took one path after another, enjoying the pond, miniature waterfall, and what seemed to be millions of plant varieties. A red bird singing in the background became the music playing while we ate our dinner.

Breaking the trip into various activities made it easier for me. In the end, the day exhausted me even with no significant ambushes. My recovery took several days, however, being with my family made the discomfort worthwhile. It was a memory I will always cherish.

On the other hand, all the days in between were monotonous. I got up, prepared whatever food I could, cleaned a little, and worked an hour here and there. The kids were a blessing to me, but I believed I was a burden to them. These feelings brought on more negative self-talk.

You are not really a mom anymore. You cannot take care of yourself, so what are you doing trying to care for these kids?

"Can you get me a glass of water?" I would often ask them. I did not always have the energy or coordination to get to the kitchen from the adjoining living room.

"Can you help me get up?" My oldest son would lend me his shoulder for balance so the Red Warrior could not attack the instant I became upright.

"Can you help me feed your brother?" John and Savannah were willing and more than capable of helping me keep food in Matthew's belly, which to this day never seems full.

"Can you help me clean?"

"Can you help me with the trash?"

"Can you?"

"Can you?

"Can you?" I became a broken record to a song I never liked from the start. I regressed from being the one the family relied on for meals, hugs, schooling, and so much more to the one continually receiving the care. My children were too young to be caregivers.

I loathed the change in roles. It seemed as if a bottle of was cod liver oil poured down my throat, but I still refused to vomit. I did not want to taste it a second time around.

MARK YOUR CALENDAR

And thou shalt have joy and gladness;
and many shall rejoice at his birth.
Luke 1:14

The time until Mark's arrival passed—one slow, long day after another. Then, on one of my visits to my midwife, Miss Sheila took Mark's measurements. She set the date to welcome this big boy into the world.

My previous deliveries had been inductions; thus, getting this one scheduled seemed routine at this point. At thirty-eight weeks, on June 23rd, the office scheduled me to go to the hospital. The upcoming week of preparations for a new baby, added to anniversary and birthday celebrations, was sure to be hectic.

First, I went home and begin packing my overnight bag, a task I postponed for too long. I could scarcely remember the items needed. However,

Robert also knew the routine by now. He proved more than able to help get the necessary supplies into my small blue suitcase and then into the vehicle. There would be no need to rush that morning and no need to add more stress. Stress seemed only to aggravate my condition and make the headaches worse.

We also put the final touches on the baby's area. We stocked up on diapers and newborn baby clothes, we brought blankets out of storage and washed them, plus a few toys, a few bottles and my breast pump just in case.

I wanted to ensure things were ready. I never told anyone, but my fear of not living through this delivery worsened with every passing moment. I feared the soldiers might win the war while I remained vulnerable and in pain. Labor and delivery are risky enough when everyone is healthy. I was not healthy.

Somehow, we always did things in groups. That week not only would the hospital induce me, but we would also celebrate our anniversary and the birthdays of two of our girls. In my life, everything does seem to happen at once.

Friday marked our fifteenth wedding anniversary. We ate a simple dinner and celebrated with a couple of hours alone. I enjoyed having a few moments in which to relax and let someone else do the cooking and dish washing. Robert and I had been through a lot in fifteen years. Somehow, we managed to stay together through all the ups and many more downs that life had thrown our way.

On Sunday, we celebrated with a small combined birthday party for Savannah and Samantha. Savannah turned seven, and Samantha became five the following day. We made a joint cake and let them open their presents at the park.

Mayors Park of Young Harris is only a quick drive from our home. It contained a playground for the kids to enjoy plus picnic tables and a gazebo. I no longer possessed the strength to chase my kids around on the grassy lawn. However, I loved watching them go on one adventure after another as their imaginations led them.

Pretending to be the T-Rex hunting prey in the jungle, John yelled, "Roar!"

"Ahhhh!" the girls screamed in unison as they scattered in different directions.

Sharon moved slower than her older siblings, and the "Stegosaurus" became the first "meal" of the day.

I experienced pure joy watching them play together and genuinely enjoy each other's company.

All of our kids were growing up much too fast. With their birthdays so close together, these two girls were often rivals. Now, there would be a third birthday in June back to back. Knowing everything the upcoming week had in store for me, made it hard to relax and enjoy these happy days. Yet, I did what I could to make our girls realize how precious they are to us and keep our apprehensions from all of them.

On the morning of Tuesday, June 23rd, we were on our way for me to check into the hospital at 9 a.m.

"Are you ready for Mark to arrive?" Robert questioned as we got into the vehicle and began our drive to town. We were alone. The kids were scattered throughout the community, spending the night with various family members and friends from church.

"I have to be," I answered as I watched the trees

out the window. I remained silent most of the drive, as fear got the best of me. As the hospital loomed closer, I kept saying silent prayers in order to keep my courage.

God, give me the strength to bring Mark into the world safely.

Lord, at least let me live to hold my baby and view Your promise fulfilled.

Lord, if it be my last day, please take me to be with You for eternity. I am ready if today is the day.

My heart raced, my blood pressure rose, and my palms became cold and clammy. I wanted to face death with courage. The time came to adorn myself with armor to win a battle against the warriors within me.

Once on the third floor of the hospital, Miss Sheila started the visit by doing an ultrasound and checking on the position of Mark.

"His head is down, and everything looks just perfect," she said to me. "I do believe Marky is ready to see the world. Is Momma ready?"

"Well, I know what to expect for the most part,

so I have to be," I replied.

Once the nurses had prepared everything for the delivery, they hooked me to every type of monitor imaginable. Then, Miss Sheila gave me a dose of Cytotec, and the wait for his arrival began.

My sister Diane came for emotional support and stayed with me during this process as well as did Robert. We tried to talk and laugh as the contractions slowly but surely increased in intensity and frequency. When the time finally arrived, the two nurses in attendance pressed on my belly from the outside. At the same time, I pushed with all of my strength to help make this delivery happen.

Finally, at 3:15 p.m., Mark Anthony Christian Dyer made his entrance into this world.

As his dad cut his cord, he shouted, "It's a boy!" while in my mind, I rolled my eyes having said this would be the case for over five years. Apparently, even the earlier ultrasound confirming a boy did not have Robert wholly convinced.

"Now do you believe what I told you?" I questioned.

"Yeah, I guess I can't deny it now that he is

here," Robert replied as proud tears welled in his eyes and rolled down his cheek, making him self-conscious.

The nurses checked my newborn baby boy.

One of them announced to everyone in the room, "He is eight pounds, nine ounces."

"Can I see him, please?" I begged.

"He does have a head full of black hair," Miss Shelia chuckled. "He looks just like his daddy. He is a beautiful baby boy. You two did good."

The two nurses attending to Mark were blocking my view of the baby I had just had. My baby. My baby, Mark. I wanted to view his face. I still didn't know if I would survive the day and I wanted to look upon his face at least once.

"Can I see him, please?" I begged again.

"He suffered a few minor bruises and his shoulder seems to be slightly sore from all the pushing. I don't think he has any other injuries," one of the nurses informed Miss Shelia.

I thanked God that Mark experienced no ill

effects from my personal war.

"We are almost done here, sweetie. We'll let you hold him in a minute," one of the nurse told me.

"Please, I want to see his face," I asked again with desperation in my voice.

The nurse finally moved over a few inches and gave me a view of his chubby little cheeks.

"He's beautiful," I said.

I laid there still wondering if I would be dead in the next few minutes. Would I hemorrhage? Would I suddenly close my eyes never to open them again? Would I have a painful seizure before I died? Would it be peaceful? I thanked God that he allowed me to view Mark's face.

His black hair and chocolate eyes look exactly as God had shown me several years earlier.

"Look, he's another little thumb sucker," Robert chuckled as Mark's tiny thumb found its way to his mouth. His older brother Matthew sucked his thumb for a few weeks after his birth and the ultrasound captured John sucking on his thumb.

As if hearing his father's words, Mark switched to sucking on his index finger. He never went back to his thumb. This habit proved hard to get him to break. Yet, he seemed more than perfect enough for me. We chuckled at his cuteness, and what seemed like defiance to his father only moments after entering the outside world.

My heart and head slowly came to realize I still lived. Hours passed and my heart still beat. My fears had not come true. I relaxed knowing the delivery was completed with no complications following it. Mark and I both made it through. I had not had any attacks. In fact, the fluid loss almost seemed to help my body equalize for the moment.

After the nurses took me to my room on the maternity ward, various family members and friends arrived, bringing my other children to meet their brand-new baby brother. Their love and affection proved he would not lack for attention from his older siblings.

"He looks like a doll, a living doll," Savannah said as she laid her eyes on Mark for the first time. "Can I hold him? Please, can I hold him?" she begged as I gave an approving nod and her dad directed her to the chair.

The kids were ready to stand in line to hold our newest addition and loved the opportunity to help care for him.

Robert and I spent the night at the hospital enjoying every moment with our new little bundle.

"Who do you think he looks like?" Robert questioned.

"Are you kidding? He looks just like you did in your baby pictures," I said with a hearty laugh. My burden eased after Mark's birth and I continued to be among the living. Joy found a place in my heart again and more of the anxiety I carried began to leave.

When we were home, I was not able to care for myself or Mark the way I had hoped. Newborns are demanding and the simplest of tasks became too much for me. Therefore, the love and attention my older children gave turned out to be a much-needed blessing.

Back when my attacks first started, I had been carrying Matthew through the house. He needed his afternoon nap and while we walked toward his room the Red Warrior sent me to the floor. I wrapped my arms tight around my child as we tumbled down.

Matthew remained unhurt, but his eyes, large as saucers, showed he received a hefty dose of adrenaline in the short trip down. This event marked the end of nap time for the day and the end of my carrying him anywhere from that point on.

I knew I would not be able to walk around with Mark as well. Newborns are more fragile and the danger in dropping them is move severe. I still needed to protect Mark from the warriors' attacks after he arrived.

Thankfully, John, our nine-year-old had strength enough to handle Matthew. As a result, he took over toting Matthew around when the little one wore himself out too much to walk. John remained a tremendous asset to the family, and he and his younger brother bonded even more as a result.

Once I had Mark, the headaches and pain became almost constant and unbearable. The relief I experienced in the hospital proved to be short lived. The warriors were back on duty, and I became physically and emotionally weak from everything the previous days brought my way.

Savannah took over carrying Mark around to get his demands met. In reality, she would have carried him everywhere if I were to let her. He became her new living doll, but I could not afford for her to forget he could be hurt and injured far easier than any piece of plastic and cloth.

I would sit down in my comfy chair and have her put Mark in my arms or allow my other children to climb onto my lap. Guilt clung to me because I could not take care of them as I desired, but, thankfully, they didn't mind at all.

Since I only worked a few hours a week, they enjoyed the extra time and attention. They did most of the fetching of supplies like diapers, clean clothes, blankets, toys and the millions of other supplies newborns use on an endless basis. All the changes and the newness of their little brother helped keep them all occupied for some time to come.

NOT SO FREE

For Israel and the Philistines had put the
battle in array, army against army.
I Samuel 17:21

In contrast to June, July flew by much faster. On July 2nd, I took Mark for his one-week checkup. He had no bruises left from his brave entrance into this world, weighed the right amount, and proved to be perfectly healthy.

"He's doing great," Miss Sheila announced after a thorough examination of my little man's health.

"I'm so glad he is," I replied. "It really worried me. I feared all of my weird problems would harm him somehow."

"Well, how are you doing now that Marky is here?" she asked with compassion as she glanced my way, taking her eyes off the wiggling baby in her arms.

"Worse," I replied.

Miss Sheila, expecting me to elaborate, turned to me and said, "How so?"

"Well, the headaches are even more frequent to the point of almost being constant. I'm dizzy a lot and absolutely exhausted," I stated, fighting back the tears.

"Being a mom with a newborn can definitely leave you exhausted," she said. "However, as for all the other symptoms, I need to talk to Dr. Breedlove and see what needs to be done next. Hop on up on this table, and I'll check your abdomen first."

After Sheila finished with my checkup, she asked the doctor to talk to me. I discussed the increase in symptoms and problems with him. He believed the sudden change in blood volume after the delivery might account for my issues. He wanted me to get extra rest, eat right, drink plenty of fluids, and tell them if my symptoms worsened at all. I did not want to mention I lived between the bed and the couch already.

Whatever I said, it had triggered little concern. Having birthed six children, I realized these were not "normal" after-delivery feelings, but I couldn't convey the right words to anyone. It seemed to be part of the Red Warrior's ability to keep the war alive inside of me.

Robert drove us home and then hurried back to his shop to finish his day. I recognized the constant interruptions were a hindrance to him. I longed to take care of everything on my own. On the inside I remained independent, while being totally helpless on the outside.

The desire for independence became another burden I had placed on my shoulders. I felt the weight of another brick pushing me farther into the depths of depression and deeper into darkness no matter how big the smile on my face appeared.

I despised appearing helpless. I despised seeming useless, and most importantly, I despised thinking of myself as a burden, and I realized I brought down my husband instead of being his helpmate.

On July 4th, our nation celebrated its freedom, but I lived like a prisoner—a prisoner in my mind, held hostage in a never-ending war.

Robert sensed my restlessness, and as we told the world good morning, he said, "Come on. Let's get out of the house. We *need* to get out of the house and enjoy this beautiful day." The sun already shone through our window.

"Mark is too little to be taking him out everywhere, and especially around people we don't know," I stated matter-of-factly.

"It's okay. We won't go where there are a lot of people around," he replied with a quick solution. "Come on. I don't want to stay inside all day," he continued, not deterred in the least.

"I don't have the energy," I said with droopy eyes and a sigh.

"Hey kids, do you all want to go to the park somewhere?" He hollered at them in the other room, ignoring my protests.

"I don't want to go out," I said in a final attempt to sound stern, knowing I had lost this battle when the kids came running into our bedroom.

"Yeah," they were all shouting and jumping around, apparently ready for an adventure.

"You may not think it is the best idea, but you need to get out," Robert looked at me with knowing eyes. "Come on, kids. I will help you get ready."

Robert always had a way of knowing when I needed the sunshine on my face. I loved to be outside but had spent most of this year indoors doing what I could and angry at not being able to do more. I remained angry at myself and sometimes angry at God without even realizing it.

Not without protest, my body got up and began the slow process of getting ready. Two hours later, we were all in the vehicle headed for a family fun day. True to his word, Robert had driven around to various spots until he found Mayors Park in Young Harris less crowded. Surprisingly, only a few other people lingered around.

We started with a picnic. Simple sandwiches and chips. The assortment proved too dull to keep young kids on a blanket in the middle of a grass field with an adjacent playground.

"Can we go play?" they would ask, one after the other.

"Eat your lunch first," I stated. "Then you can

play the rest of the day."

They grabbed a couple of bites before throwing down the rest and running. I laughed as I brought order back to the blanket and our meal.

"It is a beautiful day," I told Robert as he lay on the blanket cuddling his sleeping newborn.

"Now, aren't you glad I talked you into coming?" he said with a twinkle in his eye.

And yes, I was so glad I had gone. The sunshine seemed to send some of the depressing clouds away that had found a home over my aching head and rained negative thoughts on me. The ray of light breaking through gave me strength for the day. I enjoyed the rest of it, taking pictures or napping on the blanket with the still sleeping baby.

Once it grew dark, Robert asked the kids, "Do you all want to go get some ice cream?"

Heads bobbed in unison as if on a string. Now ice cream appeared next on the agenda for the day. We gathered all our supplies into the vehicle and started to McDonald's for ice cream cones. Then, on towards Meeks Park in Blairsville to find a suitable place to park and watch the fireworks display.

"I don't want to be too close. The fireworks might scare Mark," I said, mentioning nothing about the warrior which could also hear the fireworks and use them to start another battle in my head. It would not make sense to anyone else but me.

The local Chamber of Commerce hosted a spectacular show. We had found just the perfect place where we and one other family sat at the far end of a ball field. Together, we watched one colorful explosion in the sky after another. I took pictures of the entire thing and Mark, well, he slept through it all, not bothered by it in the least. I could count this day as a victory for me. Today, I genuinely smiled.

On the 6th of July, being Mark's original due date, I kept thinking about how different today could have been for me. However, his arrival in June made his birthday right in line with Savannah's and Samantha's birthdays for the month. It always struck me as funny how God put them together and yet gave them each their own special day. A group party would be more affordable for our family, and at the same time, each one could get individual attention on their actual birthday.

I kept thinking about how God blessed me with six children for which to care and mother. I also had the devil reminding me what a poor job I had done at both this year. He never let up.

Mother's guilt can be crippling in and of itself. My hair always looked as if I had just gotten up and threw it back or barely got the comb through it. Anything more felt too exhausting.

Housekeeping seemed more like house "losing" during the last several months—an exterior battle I had a hard time fighting. Things got left wherever the children were when they tired of the toy they were playing with at the moment. There always seemed to be some dishes in the sink that never got washed. Laundry grew into a mountain of dirty clothes.

Yes, the devil reminded me often that I seemed a hopeless case and I would never be ***good enough***... not even good enough to ask God to do any more for me.

Later in the day, interrupting my negative thoughts, Robert said, "The Gainesville Fly-in is this Saturday, and I would ***really*** like to go."

I just stared at him, not saying a word. I realized an argument would get me nowhere. As an airshow fanatic, Robert won this battle. I did not even put up a fight.

"Aw, come on. You know you will have fun," Robert continued, reaching over and tickling me, trying his best to make me crack a smile. "You know you love seeing planes, too, and this is a fly-in, so that means the crowd should be smaller." He kept on, not relenting. "I'll help with *everything*," he said with pleading in his eyes.

"I must start getting ready tomorrow if I am to have enough energy left to make it through Saturday," I replied. I let out a heavy sigh and finally smiled back at him. His excitement equaled a child who, on Christmas morning, joyfully anticipated the contents hid by colorful paper.

Traveling to this airshow would require the same supplies as the one in May plus an additional stroller, diapers, blankets, and a plethora of other necessities for a newborn. Each day, I got part of the items ready and in the vehicle. I knew the less stress and less I had to do the morning of the show, the better chance I would have of winning another victory—a merry day to remember.

On this Saturday, we ventured to Gainesville, Georgia, to watch more planes at the airport. Robert wanted to pass down his love for airplanes and teach our boys to love them as much as he does. He always wants to start them young, and no one could be younger to introduce to flying machines than Mark.

We took the day at a steady pace, and I sought shade as often as possible. Staying hydrated and relaxing seemed to help me win yet another victory. Even with a constant headache, the lack of searing pains had allowed me to enjoy yet another family outing. I fooled myself with a sense of my body healing the problems on its own.

On July 24th, we celebrated Sharon's turning three.

"What do you want to do for your birthday this year?" I asked Sharon.

"Park and cake," she replied.

"Do you want to go to Meeks Park like we did on the fourth of July?" I quizzed.

Her head shook vigorously in the negative.

"What about Mayors Park at Young Harris? The one where we had your sisters' birthday party?"

"No," she said sternly. "Different park."

"Well, then, how about Vogel State Park? We haven't been there in years. In fact, I don't think you have ever been there," I said.

"Okay," she said with glee, throwing her arms in the air and reaching for the sky. "Vogel park. Get ready!" she yelled to her siblings.

Curiously, kids want to compete, yet they want the same thing as well, so going to a different park seemed unique but still similar enough.

God blessed us again with beautiful weather and smiling, excited kids. A different park meant a different playground and a new game of make-believe.

I took my camera and began snapping shots of my beautiful children. The challenge became capturing a photo in which they were not a blur. They scampered from one spot to another, avoiding yet another dinosaur or some "bad guy" out to get them.

After one shot, I just lowered the camera, my smile lowering with it. I became utterly spent, like a car with a steady leak in the gas tank stranded on the side of the road, not reaching its destination. I ran on empty.

It seemed as if the warriors had united to defeat a common enemy—me—instead of each other. I did not experience searing pains or lost words. This round, I had not even the strength left to fall to the ground.

"Are you all right?" Robert sensed something was wrong.

I motioned a few yards away to the picnic table and put my arm in his. Leaning against him, we found our way to the bench seat.

"Do I need to take you home?" he questioned, concerned because of my sudden change.

I shook my head no and sat there on the bench. "I will not ruin Sharon's birthday. Just let me rest here for now."

Robert brought sleeping Mark in his car seat to my side and stayed in the middle of the playground with the kids.

"Can we play in the creek?" John asked as he ran up to us with Savannah close on his heels shaking her head in the affirmative.

"Ask your dad if he can walk over there with you," I managed to reply.

Off they ran as Robert agreed and followed the five of them. They loved doffing their shoes and getting their feet wet on a hot summer day. They searched for salamanders and crawfish while splashing each other with the chilly water.

Their giggles reached my ear. I sat there, a spectator to a show, one in which I should have had a co-starring role. I managed a fake smile and saved my tears for a time when I would be alone.

Not only had I lost the battle of the day, but I sensed a loss of connection, forcing myself to hide the issues from everyone I loved. Secrets kept me isolated, but the truth seemed too scary to share as if sharing made it even more real.

We finished the month with me falling deeper into depression and playing the role of spectator even more. The kids, however, kept playing their parts, growing accustomed to the missing cast member. They tried helping their dad work on equipment as Robert kept them outside with him more and more. The time passed by quickly and Mark had already turned over a month old.

I had survived the labor and delivery, much to my surprise. However, I experienced headaches more severely and more frequently. My dizziness increased as well. While I enjoyed watching my kids, I no longer felt like a mom—more like an outsider in my family.

THE CAT

As I sat and watched Robert flip the calendar over to August, I knew something had to change. I needed to shake the depression and sense of uselessness before I drowned in sorrow so deep I would be incapable of seeing the light. The solution presented itself in a pot of green. My mother-in-law, Vietta Mae, gave me a stray hosta from her flowerbed remembering I mentioned how beautiful the ones were at the South Carolina Botanical Garden.

Staring at the helpless plant made me realize it stood a far greater chance at life in the cold, cruel world outside than in a warm house, a house where its caretaker, "moi," would forget to water it one too many times, leaving its roots and finally its leaves to shrivel into nothingness as they became dust.

However, I could also do the complete opposite and, in thinking I had forgotten, water it excessively. In the end, it would give way to the root rot and die just as grueling a death. Therefore, I had no choice but to make a suitable place in which to plop this little beauty in the ground and let it show off its natural appeal.

First, I researched and found out what this species of plant needed in terms of sunlight, location, and soil. With knowledge in hand, the kids and I started working on our first project of the homeschool year—horticulture. Although our school year had not officially started, and I had no lesson plans made, getting our hands dirty marked the beginning of life lessons that year.

We chose the spot behind the house to accent our back porch and planned to outline it with large rocks for a more natural look.

"This rock?" Savannah asked, holding up a chunk of granite looking as if she would topple over at any second from the weight of it.

"That one will do beautifully," I replied. "Just don't drop it on your toes as you put it in the wheelbarrow."

We gathered three or four large rocks at a time, and John showed us his strength as he pushed the wheelbarrow up the hill and to the shady area at the back of the house. The kids ran and played while I carefully placed the rocks one after another in the shape of a semi-circle. It took me a while, but my children did not mind. They simply enjoyed the mud hole they created, which occupied them for weeks.

Day by day, we made progress. The rocks got laid in formation, topsoil dumped onto the flowerbed, and finally, a hole dug. I worked only about an hour a day, but an hour a day of accomplishment proved better than what I had been experiencing most other days.

"Can I plant it, Mom?" John questioned, seeing the moment had finally arrived.

"Absolutely," I replied as he nearly dumped the plant upside down in his excitement.

"Now, hold your hand here," I said, holding my hand on the plant to demonstrate, "around the stem as you turn the pot upside down."

"But I want to do it, Mom," John said fearfully, thinking I would do the planting as well and knowing

117

we possessed only the one plant.

"You're going to, silly," I said chuckling. "I'm just showing you how."

Then, he relaxed as he took the plant back away from me and got it out of the pot. I further instructed him on how to crunch the roots gently to help them grow out into the new soil. He got the hosta into the ground and covered it with dirt, packing the soil tightly around the baby plant.

"All done," he announced with authority.

"What can I do, Momma?" Savannah asked looking left out.

"Well, you go and get some water and Samantha can bring some mulch to go around the plant," I said, including both girls in the final tasks.

Sharon and Matthew abandoned us in favor of their puddle of mud, losing interest in anything resembling work and painting themselves and their surroundings in brown goo.

When we finished, my three helpers ran down the hill to Robert's workshop, "Daddy, Daddy, we helped Mom finish the flowerbed," Savannah yelled.

"Yeah, I got to plant the flower," John stated.

"And I watered it!" Savannah said proudly.

"And I got the mulch," Samantha chimed in.

Robert came and inspected our results. The single small hosta looked rather lonely in the flowerbed like the only shell sitting on a mile-long beach.

"I'll see if Grandma has any more hosta she might send our way," Robert said. "That one looks like it needs a friend."

Vietta May sent several over our way. Plus, Robert found a few different variations from a vendor. We filled our flowerbed with about ten hostas of various varieties and plenty of extras to start our next project.

The small flowerbed, measuring four foot by three foot, took two weeks to complete. I wanted to make flowerbeds all around the house. However, I recognized it would take me the rest of the year at the current pace.

I believed doing the landscaping would help protect me from the attacks of the Black Warrior.

After all, I wouldn't fall when I was already on the ground.

Of course, the Warrior proved me wrong. While working on one of these projects, I needed something from the shed. Halfway there, he attacked. I fell.

I fell hard and hit the edge of one of the tools on the way down, putting a long gash down my leg. I bruised from head to toe, and the wound started bleeding. As a repeat of the previous attacks, I should have been prepared. I mistakenly thought I had outwitted the Warriors. At least on this fall, Mark slept safely in his room and I didn't have to twist to protect my abdomen.

The Warriors celebrated another major victory. They knocked me down for the next few days and shadowed me under a dark, gloomy cloud of depression. The one thing—gardening—that gave me hope now gone, I felt useless while sitting around. I became trapped in my head, a prisoner of my own thoughts. My mind stopped fighting as all of its strength left.

You can't do anything right? Why do you even bother? You fail at the simplest of tasks.

Soon, we took Mark for his two-month checkup. Bruised and with a terrible headache, I walked into the exam carrying Mark in his car seat for his protection. When finished with Mark, Miss Sheila started on me, beginning with my blood pressure.

"Your blood pressure is 130 over 85. That's high for you. Are you under a lot of stress?" she asked.

"Extremely, these headaches are non-stop, and the sharp pains are now happening several times a day," I explained. "The last headache even caused me to fall and get all of these bruises and the gash down my leg." The tears started streaming down my face as I could no longer contain the emotional pain I locked away.

"Plus, it's almost time to start the homeschool year and I have nothing ready—not a single lesson written or copy of their work made. The previous two years I planned the entire school year agenda with every copy made, color coded and in order. Not to mention that we are drowning in debt." I stated between gasps. "I've only been able to complete three repairs all month. I used to do almost ten a day." When I finished, the sobbing got worse, and my mind saw no solution to the mounting list of problems.

"You poor thing," Miss Sheila sympathized with a pat on my shoulder. "I know you haven't been yourself. I'm going to get Dr. Breedlove again because you should be recovered from any effects of the delivery."

When Dr. Breedlove came in, he said, "So I hear you're not doing so well. Let's check you out."

He asked how I felt and what symptoms I experienced. He looked in my ears, down my throat, and up my nose. He checked my head and neck, every square inch of them.

"Well, I don't see anything wrong with everything I can see. I think it's time we did a CAT scan and find out if something is going on inside," he finished.

Once my exam completed, I moved to the front office and scheduled a CAT scan for two days later. In just two days—finally—we would have some answers. I feared the likely answers, but I accepted that my life ended when these symptoms began. Whatever happened, something must change.

I said in a silent prayer: "*God, I realize I have been distant lately, but please give me some answers.*

You have kept me alive this long, but I'm not really living, I want to live or I want to die. I don't want to be in limbo like this."

The nurse instructed me not to eat anything after midnight on August 20 and be at the hospital Radiology Department for the test by 8:00 a.m. I realized I could not have eaten if they told me to feast.

I arrived on schedule the morning of the test with an empty stomach and a nervous heart. In the screening room, the staff began by putting an IV in my hand.

"Now you will lie down on this bench. It is important that you stay as still as possible. In fact, if you can, it would be best for you to hold your breath during the test. It will take only a few moments, but the less movement, the better the test results," one technician stated with confidence.

I looked at the enormous donut-shaped machine while I positioned my plump self onto the table. I wanted answers. I wanted to identify what caused my problems and then I wanted it fixed. I wanted my life back, or I wanted to die. I shook my head at him and agreed, not having much of anything to say.

"Do you have any questions?" a tech asked.

"Yes, one. Do I need to stop breastfeeding Mark after this?"

"Oh, I didn't realize you were breastfeeding. Yes, the manufacturer advises not to breastfeed for forty-eight hours after receiving this contrast," the technician stated.

After connecting me to the IV containing the contrast and inspecting everything on the machine that he needed to check, he pushed me into place and left the room.

Being completely alone seemed eerily frightening. As if, for a moment, the entire world stopped breathing.

A moment later, his voice came over the loudspeaker startling me, "Okay. Get ready. When I count back from three, I want you to hold your breath until I tell you the test is complete. Three, two, one."

A whirling sound surrounded me. The machine's parts moved while I just kept a dead stare at the equipment inches above me. Whatever I did, I did not want to mess up these tests. I wanted answers.

"All finished," he said, just a few moments later.

"Wheeeew," I let out a lengthy breath.

The technician returned and unhooked the IV and stated, "We're all done."

"Did you see anything?" I asked, ready for the answer.

He stopped for a moment to think about what to say and then, not looking at me, he stated, "I have to let the radiologist read the report. Then, he will send the results to your doctor. You should learn within the next couple of days. For now, you can return to your normal activities."

Normal activities? What a joke! I spent most of my days sitting on the couch monitoring my kids or sleeping in the bed, lost in a sea of negative self-talk. This miserable existence became my new normal, and I hated it.

After being ready for answers, I must continue waiting. Two. More. Days.

Two days more than I wanted to wait. I must hold on a little longer.

Elizabeth Dyer

BAD NEWS PHONE CALL

A merry heart doeth good like a medicine: but a broken spirit drieth the bones.
Proverbs 17:22

Five little helpers crowded around me in my small and shrinking kitchen. Together, we were on a mission to make each family member a pizza of their liking. We had purchased some small crusts from the grocery store, the ingredients to make the sauce, various toppings, and cheese—lots of cheese.

I created an assembly line for hand washing and then for adding sauce to their crusts. Next, they got to add their toppings. When we were ready to finish them by adding cheese, the phone rang.

I read the caller ID—Dr. Breedlove's office. My heart skipped a beat when I answered, "Hello."

"Hello. Is this Mrs. Dyer?" the doctor

questioned.

My breath left me, and my heart seemed to be at a complete stop. Hearing a doctor's voice usually means one thing: bad news. I know the color must have left my face when Savannah looked at me and questioned, "Mom, are you okay?"

"Yes, I'm fine, sweetie," I replied. "All of you finish your pizzas." I turned and eased my way toward the living room.

"Yes, this is Elizabeth," I finally replied.

"This is Dr. Breedlove, and I'm calling because we got your test results back today. I am sorry to tell you, but they found something, a tumor," he stated and then paused.

I guess he expected some acknowledgment from me, but I had nothing to say. I needed all my courage and resolve to keep myself together. I could not fall apart in front of the children. I had been holding it in for too long.

"Are you still there?" he asked.

"Yes, I'm still here," I replied.

"Do you understand what I said?"

"Yes, I understand," I replied sounding unalarmed to ward off curious children as I wandered into my office and out of their hearing range.

"We need to schedule an MRI as soon as possible and get you an appointment with a neurologist. Can you come by in the morning?" he said.

"Yes, I will come by early," I stated.

"Good. We open at 9:00 a.m.," the doctor said. "Now, I do not want you to be alarmed. The test results do not show cancer, just a tumor. We will work with a neurologist to develop a plan of action. Do you understand?"

"Yes, I understand," I stated again keeping my voice even.

We said our goodbyes. I stood there for a moment staring out my office window. The breeze gently moved the leaves of the oak tree to and fro as if they were waving to me, trying to bring me comfort. God seemed to be sending me a message of hope with those leaves. A message saying He remembered me.

Then, I took in a deep breath, put on a brave face, and walked back into the kitchen.

"Now, is everyone done with these pizzas?" I questioned.

"Yes." "Yep." "Hey Mom, is this what you wanted on your pizza?" All the answers came, as they often do, at one time. Without further delay, I opened the door to the preheated oven, tossed in the pizzas, and set the timer.

"Who was that?" John asked me.

"Who was what?" I answered.

"On the phone."

"Oh, just some business Mom had to attend to," I reply matter-of-factly. "Nothing you to have to worry about." I touched the tip of his nose and smiled into his eyes.

However, I must not have kept my expression as nonchalant as I believed because Savannah asked for the second time, "Is everything *okay,* Mom?"

"Yes, everything is fine," I replied and forced a bigger smile on my face. "Now, let's get the table set.

Dad will be home soon, and we can eat those pizzas."

Robert got home for dinner. Soon after, we cut the pizzas and put them on the plates. During the meal, the kids kept Robert occupied with endless chatter. Each one wanted to talk about their pizza and get their moment of attention from their Dad. He responded with appropriately enthusiastic replies.

I should have been smiling and enjoying every minute, but the call from the doctor kept me preoccupied.

After dinner, we cleaned up the kitchen and headed outside to get something done before the sun hid behind the mountaintops that day. We enjoyed the sunlight from the long summer days before fall and winter came to visit us in the mountains and the days became almost unbearably short.

We wanted to work on one of our projects next to the house. The kids helped clean the yard—in their minds at least. The reality looked more like a game. They were chasing each other around with the sticks that should have been carried to the pile and screaming as if frightened of each other.

Robert kept trying to talk with me, while we

worked. "How was your day?" he asked.

"Fine," I answered. I did not want to talk about the call from the doctor's office yet.

Robert continued chattering about his day. He spoke of the chainsaws he had repaired and the ones that were frustrating.

"So, what did you get done today?" he inquired.

"Oh, just the usual," I replied and turned my attention back to the lawn.

"Are you feeling okay?"

I grew weary of hearing this question. "Fine," I replied, sounding a little short, not even looking at him and hating to continue to lie.

"Something is bothering you. What is it?"

"I'm fine." I insisted again.

"Are you mad at me or something?"

Why did he have to think my quietness had anything to do with him?

"What have I done to upset you?" he continued,

pressing me for an answer.

I turned and looked him straight in the eye. "The doctor's office called," I whispered in a stern tone.

"What did they say?" he asked loudly, too loudly for my comfort.

My eyes wide and my temper short—another change the war had caused. "I do not want to talk about it," I said through gritted teeth. My you-better-shut-up look should have been enough, but because I did not want to talk piqued his curiosity beyond what he could stand.

He crouched on the ground next to me and looked me in the eyes, taking my hands and preventing me from working on the landscaping any further.

"I have a…" I hesitated, my voice caught for a moment. "They found a… brain," I said, barely able to get the words out, "tumor."

He let go of my hands. The life left his eyes and, in its place, crept a deep sadness, fear, and hopelessness—feelings that had been my primary companion for months.

"Don't cry," I whispered. "You'll scare the kids."

Now, he took a turn at being quiet. He became the one who did not know what to say.

I heard the kids drawing in close behind us. "Time to go in, bathe and get ready for bed," I chimed with another forced smile on my face.

"Awww…" Savannah said.

"Can't we stay out just a few more minutes?" John added.

"Five more minutes, while I pick up my tools, but that's it. It will be dark soon," I said.

Robert went in the house. Alone.

BRAIN TUMORS CAN BE FUN

In every thing give thanks: for this is the will of God in
Christ Jesus concerning you.
1 Thessalonians 5:18

After getting the call from the doctor, nothing would be the same again. The call seemed to mean, "Your life is near the end, and there is nothing to be happy about."

I made things worse after the kids had gone to bed. From my office computer, I researched brain tumors online. I learned wonderful statistics such as 50 percent of the people with a brain tumor die within the first year after diagnosis. Then, of the half remaining, half of them die within five years. To me, I saw a 75 percent chance of not witnessing Mark's fifth birthday. Perhaps I would not even live to his first.

To add to my worry, I called a nurse. Someone

who worked in about every wing of a major hospital and would have some insight.

After we greeted each other, I said, "I hope this isn't a bad time to call. I had a few questions to ask after I got some news from the doctor about my results," skipping the pleasantries and getting straight to the point of my call.

"Sure. What did the doctors find out?" she asked. "I wasn't aware you had any major problems. Did something happen during the delivery?"

I went into a broad overview of my symptoms and experiences for the past few months. I realized no one except those who had witnessed an episode understood my situation, and even they did not perceive the internal battles since I had kept everything bottled inside, perhaps hoping it would just go away and be gone and done with forever.

On other days, I had believed everyone saw the war raging within me as if they were watching the Warriors battle it out on a TV screen through a looking glass mounted on my forehead.

Barely able to get the words out of my mouth, I finished, "They've diagnosed me with a brain tumor.

Can you tell me what to expect?"

"Wow! I am so sorry to hear that. How is everyone taking the news?" she asked sympathetically.

"Well, Robert and the doctor's office are the only ones who know, and I want to keep it that way. I see no reason to scare my kids, and I don't want everyone else treating me differently," I replied.

"You shouldn't go through this alone," she stated matter-of-factly. "Do the doctors want to do radiation? Or chemotherapy? Perhaps a combination of both?" she quizzed.

"I don't think so. The doctor said it wasn't cancer, just a tumor growing and putting pressure on my brain. I guess I'm glad to discover the answer," I said.

"Okay. Well, your doctors may want to do surgery to remove it," she replied. "I have worked cases where people have had brain tumors.

"The worst one was a lady about your age. They forgot to put the drain tube in her head. We told the doctor her brain was swelling, but he didn't pay attention to us in time. She died the next day. This tragedy wouldn't have happened if she had had family there insisting on her doctor's attention during her recovery.

"If they recommend surgery, you can also expect the staff will cut off all of your hair and then shave your head."

"Really?" an unpleasant image of a bald version of me popped into my head and made my stomach churn.

"Make sure you find out how many operations your doctor has done successfully. Ask lots of questions and make sure Robert is there with you during the consultation and I mean, the *whole* time. He should be coached on what to watch for and be ready to insist on immediate responses if he notices something is not right."

"Okay. Let me write all of this down," I said as I scrambled to take notes.

"You also want to make sure you go with the best in the field. You can let me know who they recommend, and I will help you research them. I won't name names, but there are some doctors I wouldn't allow to operate on me. On the flip side, there are numerous doctors at every major hospital with the needed skills, many who genuinely care about their patients and do an excellent job of treating them," she explained.

"Well," I said. "My insurance runs out at the end of this month. We don't have enough money to keep it going for me and all the kids, and no new company would take me on with this diagnosis on my charts. I don't think we'll be able to afford any type of surgery or treatment unless they do it immediately," I sighed. "I don't expect everything to fall into place that quickly."

She replied empathetically. "This is no time to be worrying about money. Get the treatment, and you can figure out how to pay for it later." And then, sounding almost angry, she said, "Your kids need their mom."

We finished the conversation with her shifting to an upbeat pep talk about getting this tumor treated so I would stay alive and get to see my kids grow up. She said everything she thought of to give me hope to no avail.

Despite this being true, I realized without any doubt I would not risk my family's entire future just to save me. How could I? They needed a house to shelter them and food to eat. An image of bill after bill coming to my family, totaling hundreds of thousands of dollars and me still dying popped into my head.

Treatments are expensive and were are poor. My family had already incurred enough debt from my inability to work for months. Robert and I resorted to using credit cards just to get by.

We were not buying anything extravagant or doing anything fancy. Our entertainment had been free—parks and airshows. Groceries were down to a minimum, and we avoided waste. We spent money on the mortgage, electricity, groceries, and a lot less in the gas tank as I was not doing on-site calls, leaving the house almost exclusively for doctor visits.

However, with the statistics showing my survival unlikely, I would not cripple my family for the rest of their lives to pay for my treatment. I stared at my notes from the phone call and all the pages of research I had printed. Grief, anger, and bitterness took over me. I sobbed. I grieved for losing what I had been until I accepted what might be—an end like Miss Ruby and my dad.

I became angry at the thought of suffering as they had and bitter because I would not see my kids mature or witness all their major life moments.

I found myself angry at God. Furious even.

God, why this! Why a tumor? If it is the end, just let it be done and over! I have no strength to keep fighting this battle.

Was I ready to die? Yes. Jesus had saved me, yet on some level, I saw myself as more dead than alive already. My health had been on a steady decline for years, and my thyroid problems left me tired. Increasing weight ate away at my self-esteem and added to my already existent knee and back problems. My suspected gallbladder issues had me on a narrow and unhealthy diet. My cholesterol began spiraling, and my energy had long since plummeted.

Yes, death seemed like an uncomplicated way out of my problems. A quick death from a heart attack, however, seemed preferable to the brain tumor. I did not want to go through surgery. I did not want my head shaved or a plate in my skull for months, maybe years.

No, death did not frighten me, but I did not want any of those treatments. The life they were describing as a best-case scenario did leave me shaking in fear. Thinking death would be easy left me with another feeling—guilt.

As a mother of six, my oldest being only nine and the youngest just two months, could I give up and leave them behind? The truth unfortunately seemed to be yes. The thought seemed selfish in some ways. However, Satan convinced me I was a negligent mother because I no longer cared for them the way I longed to. They were now my caregiver instead.

The viable treatments I had read about left me scared. I liked neither choice. I did not want to be a burden to them. In fact, I realized my life insurance policy made me worth more to them dead than alive and racking up hospital bills. At least if I died, I would provide for them financially, which had become impossible in these last few months.

I stood to leave my office, but only made it to my beige chair. I did the only thing possible. I surrendered it all to God. I understood my complete and utter helplessness. Little did I realize how mightily God would appear when I let go of everything.

As my barriers broke, I let the tears flow and my body shake with the weight of the sobs until I became physically weak. I do not know how much time had passed.

I prayed for hope instead of feeling sorry for myself and love instead of anger at how unfair life had been. A tremendous peace came over me as I turned each thing over to God. I recognized in spite of my helplessness to do anything to change the situation, God could give me a hope and a future.

I gave Him my children.

They are yours, God. Please place people in their lives to direct them toward you, even when I am gone. Let each one of them—John, Savannah, Samantha, Sharon, Matthew, and Mark—be saved and call upon Your name. Lord, let my house be called blessed because of You.

I gave him my marriage.

Lord, Robert and I have been married for many years. Please bring him peace and comfort when I am gone. Lord, help him to be the father our children need him to be. Keep him close to you and don't let him become bitter when I am gone.

Lord, keep him in church and send people from the church to surround him and give him the help he needs. Let how we treat each other be an example to others who are also suffering and facing an uncertain future.

I gave Him my current pain and any future pain.

You suffered pain for our salvation. I will look upon my pain as a privilege to serve you through it.

I release the anger I hold towards You because of this tumor and the pain I have endured. Please give me the strength to stay focused on You and not my flesh.

Lord, give me the power to glorify You no matter how much I hurt. Lord, please don't let my mind take me to those wicked places where light doesn't penetrate when I am no longer in control. Lord, keep Your light shining upon me.

I gave Him my hope.

God, my only hope is in Your promise of eternal life. Lord, thank You for sending Your son to be the ultimate sacrifice for us all. Lord, I stand on Your promise.

I gave Him my dreams.

Lord, there are so many things I want to accomplish in my life. Lord, even if I do none of them, thank You for putting the spark in my heart and soul to be more and do more.

Lord, let it carry on as a torch to my children. May they find joy in the work You call them to do. May each of them serve You with a desire in their hearts to do all things as unto You and experience peace in their minds. Let them know they are making the right decisions.

I gave Him my body.

Lord, this body is only a temporary vessel. I acknowledge I have not always taken care of it as I should. Thank You for loaning it to me, while I am here. It is Yours to do with as you want.

But, Lord, let me ask You to spare my hair if You will. It may seem vain, but I do not want my head shaved. If I am to die, I would rather be buried with my hair still on my head. Lord, You say in Your word a woman's hair is her covering and her glory. I will ask this of You. In Jesus' name. Amen.

The request for my hair to not be shaved may seem crazy to others. I laughed, too, after I prayed about it. However, I had grown my hair for over a decade, and it now measured over three feet long. If not careful, I often sat on it. My hair became part of my identity.

I did not consider myself as beautiful or even pretty, but I did not want to imagine myself with a shaved head. The thought of others looking on me in a casket with a bare head made me shudder. My children would not recognize me with no hair. Losing it seemed to be more than I could bear.

When I finished praying, I again found the joy of the Lord, and it gave me strength.

Thank you, God, for giving me this peace in my heart.

My laughter continued. I decided then and there if I were to die soon, I would not waste another moment. I did not know how many moments were left. I had spent too many hours wallowing in self-pity and anger on this day and in the preceding months.

No more! NO MORE! I told myself. Now is the

time to start having fun.

I wanted the kids to remember laughter with their mom. I tried to make others smile. I wanted other people to say I had made their lives better in some small way. I did not want to be remembered for who I had become the last few months.

I let go of all the negativity, all the things out of my control. I decided brain tumors can be fun or at least, I could have fun even if I had one.

I did not ask for healing. I did not consider myself worthy to ask, and I did not expect another miracle when I had already been granted six.

My future existed with God through salvation even if death happened to be near at this moment. My heart found peace, and I wanted to be prepared for the worst. After all, this body was not my eternal home.

Elizabeth Dyer

WHO NEEDS PRIVACY ANYWAY?

*For there is nothing covered, that shall not be revealed;
neither hid, that shall not be known. Therefore whatsoever ye
have spoken in darkness shall be heard in the light; and that
which ye have spoken in the ear in closets shall be proclaimed
upon the housetops.*
Luke 12:2-3

Robert secured a babysitter the night before—his mom and dad. A knock on the door early in the morning alerted us to their arrival, just after 8:00 a.m. as Vietta Mae walked in moving much faster than Wayne. The kids were up, but still sleepy. I cooked breakfast, trying not to be sick as nervousness overtook me regarding this visit to the doctor.

Vietta Mae started out asking, "Why do you have to go to the doctor's office now?"

"Oh, it's nothing," I said with a genuine smile on my face, focusing on not getting burned as I finished the morning meal.

"I don't understand why they need to see you so early. Not after Mark is already here and doing so well," she continued.

The kids were looking our way big-eyed, no doubt wanting some answers I would not give them.

Robert came into the room dressed and ready to go. His mom started asking him the same questions. They disappeared into my office, and I no longer heard the conversation. As Vietta Mae walked back into the kitchen, she tapped my shoulder and said, "I'm so sorry."

"I will be okay no matter what happens," I told her, still smiling. Whispering, I added, "Please don't say anything in front of the kids."

I left her to divvy the food onto the kids' plates as Robert and I headed out the door to get the MRI on schedule. We passed his dad headed into the house. I perceived this would be the end of my treatment making this task pointless. However, I wanted to make everyone feel like they were helping. I had come to terms with the situation, and I must give everyone else time to adjust.

Once in the vehicle, I spoke with Robert. "You *told* your mom?" I stated with an accusing and questioning tone.

"Yeah, I figured she needed to know, and she insisted. She thought something was wrong with Mark," he added.

"What part of I don't want ***anyone*** to know did you not understand?" I finished with sarcasm and a touch of anger. "I would have preferred if you didn't have to learn of the diagnosis, but who would drive me to these appointments if not you?"

Robert drove the rest of the way with a stunned look on his face. He acted differently, and suddenly I found myself in the middle of the exact scenario I wanted to avoid.

When I walked into the doctor's office, we skipped the usual wait. The receptionist directed us straight to the door and to the pleasant lady sitting behind the small desk covered in paper sorters. From the looks of her surroundings, her job seemed to comprise of scheduling appointments outside of their office and dealing with lots of paperwork. She called the hospital and told them the procedure the doctor ordered—two MRI scans of my brain one with and one without contrast.

I still felt uneasy at the thought of the entire procedure, but I wondered where the fear came from. The doctor had diagnosed me with a brain tumor already. Why be afraid? Did I expect the scans would show I did not have any brains in there? The image of doctors staring in shock at a blank skull made me giggle, and the staff and other patients gave me a curious look.

During this time, Miss Sheila walked by, chart in hand. Seeing us, she stopped and asked in her usual cheerful fashion, "How is our little Marky doing?"

"Wonderful," I replied. "Growing super-fast and changing every day."

"Babies have a way of doing that," she replied with a giggle. "What about you? Did you get the test results back?"

I nodded and whispered, "Tumor." I still hated the sound of the word.

"Oh dear," she said with a heavy sigh, and she came and hugged me. "My kids and I will all be praying for you."

"Thank you," I said, knowing they would, in fact, be praying. Her steadfast faith had never wavered in all the years since I met her.

They scheduled the scan for August 27 at 9:30 in the morning. I breathed a sigh of relief as if I had held my breath since the doctor called with the news. We were now free to go. Having gotten the test scheduled, I realized my stomach growled from hunger. Robert concurred with a like growl from his abdomen, so we grabbed some breakfast at the local Waffle House.

As we scanned the room in order to find a seat, we saw Sam, my computer repair client, his wife, and grandson sitting in a booth. I had not seen Sam since the day I lost my memory while installing his repaired computer at his home.

"How are you all doing?" I asked with a cheery smile on my face.

Sam grinned as his grandson climbed all over him. "We're doing well. How are you?" Before I could answer, he asked, "Oh, and I'm glad I ran into you. One fan in my computer has started making a noise. Can you fix it?"

"Yes, of course, that shouldn't be a problem. I have several types of fans in stock. When would you like us to pick it up?"

"Tomorrow would be great," he stated. Robert and I looked at each other quizzically. "Or today. We are going home after we finish eating."

"That will work," I replied. "We should be able to fix it today and bring it back tomorrow."

Sam added, "Did you ever get any results from the doctor?"

I couldn't answer. I would not make myself repeat the word. The smile left my face.

Sam asked, "Is everything okay?"

I shook my head no, unable to give an audible response.

"I'm so sorry to hear that," he said. His wife giving me a sympathetic look.

"Thank you," I finally managed.

We finished eating, with me focusing on the positive things and a lot less on myself and this issue.

We enjoyed our breakfast and our time together, but soon started toward Sam's house and then back home.

On the drive, I got a call from a lady at church. "We found out you have a brain tumor," she said. "What can we do to help? We have the prayer chain going but is there anything else we can do to help you and your family?"

"You *know*? How did you find out? I didn't think anyone had been notified," I replied, shocked at the call.

"Vietta Mae called and put you on the prayer chain. We are all praying for you and praying for a miracle," she stated.

"Well, thank you so much," I replied, overwhelmed and confused. I did not want a lot of people treating me differently. I had witnessed it before, how everyone suddenly wants to make peace or act like they are walking on eggshells around someone terminally ill. Death with dignity and grace and *alone* would be preferable to me.

When we got back home, while Robert unloaded Sam's computer, I asked Vietta Mae, "Did you tell anyone about my condition?"

"Well, I put you on a prayer chain with the church," she said looking confused. "Was that not okay?"

"I had wanted no one to know," I replied.

"This is no time to worry about that. You need prayer, all the prayer you can get, and those kids need their momma," she stated. She defended her actions and looked at me as if the tumor had already made me lose my mind. Perhaps it had. I was not quite sure.

The world now learned of my condition and therefore, meant I must do the one thing I absolutely did not want—tell my kids. We needed to tell them before they received the news from someone else. I asked Robert to be there and help me. I tried to make light of it and not let the kids think my death could happen at any minute. The mind of a child has a way of exaggerating things, especially if they are scared.

We gathered all the kids together in the living room. All of them, except Mark, sat in my or Robert's lap. Mark slept peacefully in his crib and would understand none of it anyway.

God, please give me the right words to say to my

children, so they are not frightened.

I began, "I realize you guys have noticed Mom has been overly clumsy lately and had a lot of headaches." They shook their heads in the affirmative, not wanting to interrupt. "Well, I went to the doctor the other day, and they diagnosed me as having a tumor in my head. I will go for another test in a few days, and after that, we'll figure out the next step. We will keep taking steps according to what they find. I do not want any of you to be scared. God's got this under control."

I did not desire to elaborate any further. The kids all gave me hugs and kisses, telling me I was going to be okay. I kept smiling, and the fact I did not cry probably helped them handle the situation as well.

John suddenly chimed, "Mom, let's all pray for you. Can we?" John led his brothers and sisters in a sweet prayer for me, *"Dear God, please take care of our mom. We love her very much. Make her head better. Amen."*

"Amen," we all agreed.

During the next two days, we started receiving one call after another. Our phone rang more than in all the years of our marriage. In addition, we received several visits from fellow church members including the pastor, a few deacons, and some friends.

I received e-mails and messages from people I knew and loved, but also from many strangers. God started showing me how much others loved me and how much love I could share with others. He also showed me *how* to love others in their time of need.

Some relatives we had not seen in a while stopped to visit. Lots of people brought food, which blessed us during this time as I cooked so little these days and we experienced no time between visitors for such tasks.

All the company occupied me to the point the kids' actions and their emotional state lost my attention. They were enjoying eating the food brought over, especially the Domino's pizza. They took their time picking off every single olive, pepper, and onion to get it down to just cheese and pepperoni, the only way they believed pizza should be served.

My children apparently understood only bits and pieces of various conversations as they darted from room to room. Savannah, confused by the volume of visitors, asked John, "Why are so many people coming over?"

John answered, "Because Mom's about to die and everybody wants to say goodbye."

Overhearing their comments, I walked into the hall and said, "John, no they are not! Everyone's coming over to pray, and no one knows what will happen." I gave them both a hug. "Keep praying like you did when we told you. God will listen to you." Although I believed death was near, I did not want the kids expecting my end or focusing on it. Realizing they already believed this left me shocked and uncertain on what to do next.

"Robert, we need to speak to the kids again tonight and give them hope no matter what happens to me," I said. "John assumes everyone is coming to say goodbye before I die."

As our house finally emptied of guests, we gathered to pray and talked to the kids some more. We had to hold on to hope. At least, they needed to hold on. I would not have them sinking into depression or bitterness because of me.

I already faced that ugly demon of a dark cloud, and I did not want them to see the darkness. I wanted them to enjoy every moment left that they experienced with me and remember it all fondly.

ASKING FOR PRAYER

*And this is the confidence that we have in him, that, if
we ask any thing according to his will, he heareth us*
1 John 5:14

As the afternoon slipped into evening on
Wednesday, I finally found some alone time to pray,
and God directed me to make my situation public.

Public!

What? That can't be right. God knew I wanted
to hide it, not make it known publicly—even more
than it already was. I did not want anyone else's pity.
I did not want friends or family to act weird or
different around me. I yearned to keep my secret. Yet
God said otherwise.

Therefore, to be obedient, I ventured online and
began setting up a Facebook account. Although the
social media website had existed for some years, I

did not desire an account, but here I was.

My first Facebook post at 5:46 p.m. on August 28, 2009: "I got a call from the doctor on Monday. He says I have a brain tumor.... so tomorrow I go back to UGH [Union General Hospital] for an MRI. Please keep me & my family in your prayers!"

A few people had already accepted a friend request from me after the contact upload feature, and I saw six promises of prayer by the end of the evening.

On to Twitter I continued. Going through the same process of creating a new account and following some people, I typed my first tweet. "On Monday, I got a call with my test results, and the doctor says I have a brain tumor. I have chosen to praise God through all of this!"

On Twitter, something else happened that I did not expect. Other people with brain tumors found my post and communicated with me. I realized how many people shared this ordeal. I did not desire to share my diagnosis of a tumor, but connecting with those in similar circumstances brought me comfort difficult to explain.

As some of them communicated with me privately, discussing the symptoms and procedures they already experienced, I found others who understood my war and all the battles I fought. I discovered the Black and Red Warriors launched attacks against others, even if those individuals called them by another name.

Once I finished online, time was insufficient for our usual Wednesday night routine so, we scurried to leave for church service if we were to have any chance of making it on time. The kids got ready for the weekly Kids' Stuff program or for the most part just went as they were. They needed a mental break from the day, and so did I.

In previous years, I had helped gather, purchase, or even create the props for the plays the group did. I remember searching frantically for a toy skunk for one of the productions.

One of my favorite tasks—the French hats I sewed—no pattern, just a picture and an idea. I made them according to my best guess, and they were fantastic—far better than I expected or believed possible.

During another week, I watched *Star Trek* to

create lookalike costumes for two cast members. Afterward, I still watched the show, enjoying the sci-fi series with Robert.

This year, I only served as a spectator—watching everyone else living life—banned from the action because of the war raging in my head.

With everyone at the church knowing my *"secret,"* I got to spend virtually no time watching the program. Instead, many church members, one after another, took time to minister to me and pray for me. Many shared stories of family members who had survived cancer or brain tumors and stories of others who had moved into remission with no more signs of the disease, or of some who had passed on to glory.

I especially remember Pastor Bill and his wife, Bobbie. They were and are such a Godly example to others. They prayed with me and loved on me. I have always admired them and their love for the Lord.

I remember listening to Bill's teachings from the pulpit and learning so much from what he shared, and Bobbie, a kind and gentle soul, proved impossible not to love.

I also prayed with Chuck, their son, and Barbara, their daughter-in-law, in addition to some members I had never met before. I realized God put me in their hearts and on their minds. Their prayers and sharing their experiences and love brought comfort to my soul.

I still failed to pray for God's healing, but many other people did. At this point, God took me from hiding to sharing, and asking for prayer. People shared stories of how I had positively affected their lives. The stories brought me an unexplainable joy. And knowing they helped carry my burden and lifted it from my shoulders brought me further into peace and acceptance.

I did not sense the pity I expected and instead found relief, friendship, the love of God, and hope for my future whether here on Earth or in eternity.

My kids witnessed how many people were rallying for us, and it brought peace to them. I wanted them to stay part of a church family with or without me. I prayed Robert would keep taking them to church in my absence.

As the program closed, Reeda Faye, a dear friend from church, walked up to my seat and spoke to me, "Penni and I want to come to your home and pray with you tonight. Would that be okay?"

"Absolutely," I replied.

I knew them both well from our Mommy Time Group that used to meet once a week to read a faith-based book, eat lunch, and pray. The group had stopped meeting a little over a year before, but I remained close with many of the ladies.

They arrived at our house not long after we came home. Robert took the kids downstairs for their baths and bed while I visited. We quickly dispensed with the pleasantries and addressed the purpose of the visit. Both were mothers with waiting families at home.

"We were reading Hebrews 11 on the way over here," Reeda Faye began. "Now faith is the substance of things hoped for, the evidence of things not seen."

"Yes," Penni stated. "I love that Scripture."

"God wants your faith strong through all of this," Reeda Faye continued, speaking as one with authority.

"I do have faith," I replied. "I'm not afraid of

what all is about to happen to me. I know where I am going if I die, and I've given my children to God. I pray God keeps faithful people in their lives if He calls me home. I hope both of you will help minister to them if I'm not around."

"Good," Reeda Faye replied, reflecting on my words. "We want to anoint you with oil and pray over you. Is there somewhere we can go for privacy?"

"Yes, we can go to my office," I replied.

When we moved into the other room, they sat me in my comfy beige chair that had become such an important part of my life during these past few months.

"Elizabeth, we have already prayed for protection over ourselves. Are you ready?" Reeda Faye asked.

"Yes," I replied, not sure what to expect.

"Good. I will anoint you with this holy oil we have brought just as they did in Bible times to cast out demons and heal the sick."

They stood and anointed my forehead with oil in the shape of a cross. Then they lay their hands on my head. In all my years of being a Christian and taking part in prayer, this became the first time I experienced anointing.

When they prayed, they asked for my deliverance from a demonic spirit, not for healing. They requested for God to break the bond of rejection from both my heart and mind.

This spirit had begun attacking me when I was young. As a child, I always seemed less than—not good enough. I made straight A's and my mom would simply reply, "That is what we expect."

I cleaned and organized, but there always came another task needing completion—never praise for what I had already accomplished. Her reply would be, "Now go clean the kitchen some more." Or "Go and clean your room."

Regardless, of how hard I tried, I still fell short. What I did never seemed good enough; therefore, in my mind, I would never be good enough.

After my father's death, I never heard from any of my father's side of the family as I grew into adulthood. My mother stated they did not want me. They did not think of me as family and did not love me. I felt rejected.

The dissension between my mom and her various relatives also left me orphaned from her side of the family as well. To have so many relatives, I seemed to have no family. Something must be wrong with me. No one wanted me around, I thought.

Although not consciously aware of this demonic presence in my life, the fear of rejection led me to reject others first before they had the opportunity to reject me. In retrospect, the fear damaged a lot of relationships that could have been genuine friendships. Nothing could be undone now, but I could see things differently for the future.

I knew God already loved me, but the spirit of rejection weighed upon me for years. I just accepted that no one loved me, and I became unlovable. After all, *I did not love myself.* Why would anyone else love me?

Reeda Faye began praying louder:

Dear Father, we lift up Sister Elizabeth to You today Lord. Rejection has bound her for far too long. Today, we are binding and casting out the spirit of rejection from her in the name of Jesus.

Yes, Lord. Penni echoed.

God, we are following Your word and asking her to be free and Your Holy Spirit to come into her heart and dwell in the space that rejection took up.

Yes, Lord.

God, if she is being tormented by any other ungodly spirits, we bind them and cast them out as well. Lord, we do not have to know their names for You know. Oh, God.

Yes, Lord.

We bring all of this before You in the name of Jesus. Amen.

Amen and Amen.

The prayers were the opposite of what I expected but were what I needed. As I prayed, I became released from something that had burdened me. By the time they finished praying, I sobbed again the same as the day I received the diagnosis. The release seemed the same as when I prayed, putting everything down at God's feet. Another set of chains loosened and fell away. How amazing freedom feels!

Reeda Faye quoted John 8:36. This verse became one of my favorites.

If the Son therefore shall make you free, ye shall be free indeed.

Another veil that shadowed my mind disappeared. The Warrior of Rejection experienced a major defeat in this moment.

Rejection is the most powerful of all the demonic spirits. After all, it is what caused others to deny and then crucify Christ. The Spirit of Rejection keeps many people bickering with each other and turning their backs on those in need. Rejection tears families apart and leaves others with broken hearts. Rejection leads to abuse and self-harm.

Everyone in this world has experienced rejection, but some, like me, become burdened with it even before their birth and battle it their entire lives.

Elizabeth Dyer

PSALM 34

Ask, and it shall be given you; seek, and ye shall find;
knock, and it shall be opened unto you: For every one that
asketh receiveth; and he that seeketh findeth; and to him that
knocketh it shall be opened.
Matthew 7:7-8

After Reeda Faye and Penni left, I continued praying, still crying, and sitting in my beige chair with my Bible open in my lap. However, I could not read through my tears. At this point, they were not tears of self-pity but of relief and release.

The phone rang. Reeda Faye called, while Penni drove. "Penni and I prayed some more, and we sense God is giving you the promise in Psalm 34. Get your Bible and read the Scripture."

As I turned my attention to my Bible in my lap, which I realized already lay open to Psalm 34. I then replied to them, "I couldn't agree more." I hurriedly hung up the phone to fully ingest the words before me, neglecting even to say goodbye.

I read the verses out loud to myself and praying through each verse.

Psalm 34, King James Version (KJV)

[1] I will bless the Lord at all times: his praise shall continually be in my mouth.

Yes, Lord, I will bless You and I will praise You. I want others to know I am Your follower by everything I do and say.

[2] My soul shall make her boast in the Lord: the humble shall hear thereof ,and be glad.

Oh, yes, Father! I cannot boast about anything that has happened to me. I can only give the glory to You. If my words make others praise you and experience joy, all the better.

[3] O magnify the Lord with me, and let us exalt his name together.

Lord, may everyone that hears of my story rejoice in all You did for me this day. May I be able to help fight the spirit of rejection with others so they, too, can experience true freedom.

4   I sought the Lord, and he heard me, and delivered me from all my fears.

Yes, Lord! I can finally live without the fear of rejection. I can live without fear of death. I cannot imagine what I can do if I go boldly forth and not worry about how others perceive me or what they think of me. I cannot imagine how I can view myself with the self-hatred gone and your love in its place.

5   They looked unto him, and were lightened: and their faces were not ashamed.

With rejection gone, shame is leaving, too! There is no shame in loving the Lord and letting others know it. May our face shine Your light for others to see.

6   This poor man cried, and the Lord heard him, and saved him out of all his troubles.

Lord, you saved me from so many troubles. Not just tonight, but throughout my entire life. Lord, thank you for being there for me even in times when I drew away from You. You are forever faithful. Lord, help me to always seek you first in times of trouble.

7   The angel of the Lord encampeth round about them that fear him, and delivereth them.

Lord, thank you for sending your angels to protect me and deliver me from any harm. Lord, they are your soldiers and they are far mightier than the evil warriors I have been losing battles against. Forgive me for not asking you to fight this battle for me sooner.

8   O taste and see that the Lord is good: blessed is the man that trusteth in him.

Lord, I am blessed. May others always call me blessed and may they know my trust is in you and all of my blessings flow from you. Lord, I trust you with everything I am and everything I have.

9   O fear the Lord, ye his saints: for there is no want to them that fear him.

Lord, the only fear we should have is of you. For you are the almighty. No one and nothing else has the power of Heaven and Hell. Lord, my fear of you protects me from all other harm. May I always fear You and conquer all other fears with Your help and through Your power.

10   The young lions do lack, and suffer hunger:
but they that seek the Lord shall not want any
good thing.

*Lord, you provided me with so many good
things. Beautiful children, a home, a family to call
my own, friends who love me and pray with me, and
so many more things that I did not even know I
needed. Thank you, God, for being my provider.*

11   Come, ye children, hearken unto me: I will
teach you the fear of the Lord.

*Lord, let my children learn to fear You and
follow You all the days of their lives.*

12   What man is he that desireth life, and loveth
many days, that he may see good?

*Lord, I desire a life that glorifies You for
however many days You appoint for me. May the rest
of my days be a testimony to others.*

13   Keep thy tongue from evil, and thy lips from
speaking guile.

*Lord, help me to see the best in people and speak
words that build them up. Lord, help me guard my
tongue from attacking anyone in anger or bitterness.*

Lord, You created everyone as a masterpiece. Let me always see the beauty in others, so I may reach past the darkness and help show them the light.

¹⁴ Depart from evil, and do good; seek peace, and pursue it.

Lord, I want my life to be spent in peace and I always want to pursue peace for it is the only way to live in harmony with others.

At the same time, I want to cast away all evil deeds and thoughts and seek to do good for others as you did for me.

¹⁵ The eyes of the Lord are upon the righteous, and his ears are open unto their cry.

Lord, thank You for Your watchfulness and for hearing my prayers. Thank You for sending comfort in my times of trouble.

¹⁶ The face of the Lord is against them that do evil, to cut off the remembrance of them from the earth.

Lord, please never turn from me and always correct my path if I begin to stray. If my words can ever lead someone to You, please give me the words to reach their hearts and minds so they may not be cast into the pit.

For the heartaches someone causes here on Earth are only temporary while Heaven and Hell are eternal.

17   The righteous cry, and the Lord heareth, and delivereth them out of all their troubles.

Thank you again, Lord, for delivering me from my many troubles, especially those that were unbeknownst to me.

18   The Lord is nigh unto them that are of a broken heart; and saveth such as be of a contrite spirit.

Lord, you broke me and put me back together as a potter and his clay. Thank You, Lord, for healing my broken heart and loving me more than I ever understood before.

Lord, thank you for making me feel whole and wholly loved by you. Thank you for accepting me as I am.

19   Many are the afflictions of the righteous: but the Lord delivereth him out of them all.

Lord, you never promised any of us an easy life. I am thankful You are here with me through all of these trials even when I grew angry. Even when I seemed to turn my back on you, Lord, you delivered me from all of those feelings and kept my heart from bitterness.

20   He keepeth all his bones: not one of them is broken.

Lord, thank you for the prophecy of Your son and His time here on this Earth so we might spend eternity with You. Lord, thank you for sending Jesus Christ to fulfill each and every prophecy. Thank you for Your sacrifice for my salvation.

21   Evil shall slay the wicked: and they that hate the righteous shall be desolate.

Lord, I never want to be one of those people. Thank you for protecting me from them. If an opportunity should arise to turn one such person away from their evil ways and to seek you, please give me the words to reach them.

22   The Lord redeemeth the soul of his servants: and none of them that trust in him shall be desolate.

Thank you for salvation and for all those You bring to salvation. Although I am unworthy, You accepted me. Lord, I love You. I thank You for accepting sinners like me and turning us into saints.

I read Psalm 34 over and over again that night until Robert dragged me to bed. I loved the words and committed them to my heart, but not yet understanding how they would play out in my life, however many days I had left.

The words also gave me hope. God had some use for me yet. I could make some impact in whatever time I would be given.

I would be able to praise His name through my circumstance. God would continue to provide for my family and me. God was transforming me into a better person. God gave me hope.

Hope.

Everlasting Hope and now it was fully and wholly mine.

LOOKING BACKWARD AND FORWARD

I will remember the works of the LORD: surely I will remember thy wonders of old.
Psalm 77:11

The next morning I was awake unusually early—far earlier than necessary for the test at 9:30 or to fix breakfast or anything else. I assumed if I arose, I would wake all the kids and create a grumpy little bunch that their grandparents would rather not deal with.

My solution was to lie there with my thoughts racing faster than my mind could comprehend.

I rolled onto my back and found Robert staring at me. Apparently, he could not sleep through the night either. We lay there for the next hour or two whispering to each other about all the wonderful things that had happened in our lives.

183

"Do you remember, when we first got married and lived in the 'round house,' it seemed we had no privacy," Robert stated.

"Yeah, every neighbor wanted a view of the pond in our backyard—and it seemed a view of our living room as well," I added. "Do you remember the overly friendly neighbor? I sure didn't miss him after we moved."

"No. I'm so glad we now have a place with more breathing room."

"Yeah, the other location benefited us when I drove across the mountain for college though. It seemed like a long two years when we lived there."

"I'm glad we moved when we did. The new owners added two more houses to the tiny lot. There would have been no privacy after they built them and no peace and quiet during the process."

"I never imagined we would end up building our own home. Did you?" I asked.

"It proved to be a bigger project than even I imagined," Robert replied. "We lucked out getting to live in the garage apartment up the road less than a mile away while we were working on it."

"It was handy. It would not have been possible to work those late nights and get it done in the two years it took us if we would have had further to drive."

"Yeah, working until three o'clock in the morning and then getting up at for work about killed me."

"Don't forget, I still attended college and drove over the mountains on the weekends," I added. "I worked with you until about midnight each night and had to come home and do all of my homework for school. I still can't believe I kept my GPA at four-oh with all we had going on."

"That's because you are so smart," Robert smiled.

"Well, I have not seemed smart since this tumor started growing," I sighed. "I can barely fix a computer these days."

"It was only a month after we finished the house that you found out you were pregnant with John," Robert chuckled. "I'm sure glad we got the house done first."

"Yeah," I said. "Do you remember how you

wouldn't speak for three days after I told you? I should have been the one in shock. I had been told I couldn't have children and here I stood holding a positive pregnancy test."

"I remember counting all of his fingers and toes after he was born."

"Our beautiful blonde-haired, blue-eyed boy," I said, smiling. "What do you think he will be when he grows up?"

"I don't know. Maybe a preacher. He looks like a preacher when we go to church on Sunday, and he has strong faith in the Lord."

"Yes, I pray he never loses his faith. He is a powerful leader," I added. "I also envision him being a politician and fighting to uphold strong moral values. We really need leaders willing to stand up for what's right. What helps everyone, not just what helps themselves."

"I could also see him being a judge or a police officer."

"Of course, he loves his planes and he might want to join the armed forces, especially the Air Force."

We continued discussing each of our children and what they might be one day…

We suspected that Savannah, our brown-haired, chocolate-eyed girl, would become a nurse or a doctor. She loved to care for her baby dolls, not just as if she were their mother, but as if they needed extra care and attention. Savannah pretended to give them shots if they were sick or helped them with medicine so they would be all better in no time.

She also has an artistic side and loves to draw with amazing detail. However, she also assumed she had to be unique in every way. In her mind, none of her brothers and sisters should be allowed to like the same things she did. This put an unfortunate barrier between her and her siblings who liked to do things together.

Samantha, our dark-haired, hazel-eyed girl, loves to spend time alone. She would often be in deep thought or drawing and coloring. She definitely has an artistic mind that shows in all she does. She has a flair for style and design. We assumed she would be an artist or famous clothes designer, or she might also own an island full of every type of monkey. She would create a map to go on a "Pic Dora" adventure (aka Dora the Explorer, her favorite cartoon).

However, she is highly sensitive and seeks the approval of others, especially her older sister. I pray Samantha becomes confident in who she is in Christ and seeks His approval alone.

Sharon, our blonde-haired, hazel-eyed, animal-loving daughter, would take in every stray animal along the way, carrying it around, loving and hugging it nonstop. She wants to make pets of all of them, from lizards to dogs to cats to frogs. We expected Sharon might well be a veterinarian or a curator at a zoo.

She might also be a naturalist or park ranger, anything that would allow her to be around animals. Even when drawing with her sister, she almost always drew animals.

Matthew, our brown-haired, blue-eyed middle boy, had a strong build even at an early age. Many people called him a future football player when they would see him. We envisioned him joining the military, playing a sport, or anything that required the strength of both heart and muscle. I prayed his heart would always focus on Jesus first.

With Mark being so young, we did not guess what kind of work he might enjoy. Therefore, we talked about how he might look as he grew older.

We laughed about how much Mark looked like Robert with his black hair and dark brown eyes. The photographs Vietta Mae showed us of Robert as infant which could easily be mistaken for Mark. Would he also enjoy working on equipment like his dad?

My thoughts wandered to whether my time left would allow me to see any of these developments. I did not expect I would.

My heart broke at the thought, and Robert held me while we both sobbed. I would do anything for my kids, including sacrificing my health or my life. The thoughts of what might happen to them once I left forever overwhelmed me.

I experienced what it felt like to lose a parent so young and how it affects children for the rest of their lives. I wanted better and more for my children than I ever had.

Soon, the alarm clock signaled it was time to arise and move forward. We went through a similar procedure as before, getting breakfast ready and letting my in-laws inside as we headed out the door.

Elizabeth Dyer

MRI—MY REALLY IMPORTANT MOMENT

For we walk by faith, not by sight
2 Corinthians 5:7

At the hospital, the nurse inserted an IV in my left hand—the opposite hand used for an IV infusion before I underwent the CAT scan---then my hands matched. This small detail brought me an inkling of comfort that at least they would match as I lay in my coffin. When the nurse was finished, she directed me to a room down the corridor and to the left.

My feet seemed as if someone had tied weights to them, the weight of knowledge of my impending death and the meaningless ordeal I was going through at the time. Had Robert not been by my side, arm-in-arm, I do not know if I would have made it the short distance.

The radiology technician met us in the waiting room for the MRI. Clipboard in hand, he instructed me in a robotic tone, "Leave all your jewelry, your purse, and anything metal in those lockers over there. I will give you a few minutes while we get everything ready for your test. You are having a head scan done, correct?"

"Yes," I replied. "The test is for the brain tumor."

I had brought nothing with me except the glasses I wore. I knew I wouldn't need them once I was dead, but I thought about how I wanted to be buried with them. I had worn glasses since I was a young girl and they had become a part of me.

As the tech left, a void and silence entered. He left us to wait as he prepared for us, more specifically, me. Robert's being there helped me to act brave. I could not fall apart and start bawling, or he would do the same.

I found myself without the strength to talk, and Robert seemed the same way. We had already said everything that morning. I had left all my happy thoughts of my children at home and now could think of nothing more than the end. My end.

Moments later, the technician appeared again, "We are ready for you now, Mrs. Dyer. Step into this room." I wondered if his white scrubs and methodical matter-of-fact tone were not adding to my dread.

I handed Robert my glasses, and he squeezed my hand as if it would be the last time he saw me. I blindly followed the technician into the testing room, hoping I would not trip along the way. The Black Warrior would not even have to attack to make me fall if the tech walked fast enough for me to lose sight of his blurry figure. The tech who was so focused on his work did not seem to realize how much I depended on his blurry figure.

I entered the testing room. It felt cold and unfriendly. A chill set in that went down to my bones. Nothing was friendly in this room. The large off-white machine that was to provide answers, the gurney on which I was to be placed and the stand which held the dye that would later be pumped into my veins provided function and no comfort.

"Lie down here," he instructed. "Now, scoot up so that your head fits right in here."

Once in place, he strapped my head into an

immovable brace. The sense of being trapped took over. I hated feeling held down. Therefore, I prayed: *God, help me stay calm during this test. No one had told me that the test required the tech to strap me down. I dislike this sensation, but I do not want to mess the test up. Please give me peace to get through.*

The technician must have sensed my tension when he asked, "Are you all right, ma'am?"

I tried to nod, but the straps prevented me, to my dismay. "Yeah," I finally squeaked out.

"Okay, good," he replied, doing everything in well-trained rapid movements. "This is your first round of tests. We will run these without contrast or dye. When this set completes, I will use the IV to put the contrast in your system and do the entire process over again."

"What if I'm allergic to the dye?" I questioned.

"That would be extremely unlikely," he replied. "Here are your earplugs. It will get loud in there. I need you to put these in snuggly." As I took them in each hand and began moving them toward my ears, he continued, "This will take considerably longer than the CAT scan test. I will need you to stay as relaxed as possible during the test. Just breathe normally. Are you ready?"

"Yes," I said stuffing my ears with the protectors. I was ready for this test and spiritual trial to be over ... ready to simply die and be done with this before I turned into someone else.

Not convinced, he added, "If you need the test to stop for any reason, holler. I will be in the other room, but I can still hear you."

"Thank you," I replied. I remained determined to get this finished as quickly as possible and I had no intention of making it stop midway to calm my nerves.

At that moment, I became angry at myself, not knowing why I had bothered to even come for this test. The considerate, yet focused technician slid all 312 pounds of me, into the tiny hole of an enormous MRI machine. My lack of sleep and stress level made it seem way too early in the morning to handle the situation.

A casket is bigger than this machine and the diagnosis I received would have me in one soon, I thought.

I began dealing with an unrealized fear of compact spaces and loud noises—claustrophobia and phonophobia slapped me in the face. I had never experienced either before. Then again, I had never been in a comparable situation in which I imagined myself being buried alive. I felt death approaching while I was unable to move.

Cramped, miserable, and ready for this traumatic experience to be over, I fought to keep myself together. The machine sounded like hundreds of machine guns firing at my head even through the earplugs. The level of noise proved unbearable for me. Yet, if I moved, the test would be ruined and would have to be started over. I reminded myself that I had to remain still at all costs.

Calm down, I repeated to myself again and again.

I closed my eyes and silently prayed and prayed and prayed. I tried to imagine my favorite places, enjoying time with my favorite people, and other joys. I attempted to make complete thoughts. Between the pressure from the tumor and the never-ending banging noises from the machine, none of my ideas seemed coherent.

It took all my effort not to go into a full-blown panic attack. I had never experienced one, but I also had never experienced a brain tumor either. Maybe the circumstances entitled me to panic this once.

Despite the fan placed at my feet, the temperature was above miserable. The coldness of the room had turned to extreme heat. To make matters worse, the breeze annoyed me by blowing a lone strand of hair back and forth across my face continually. I dared not move to get the hair out of the way, and it seemed like it tickled me for hours—a torture technique, perhaps.

Yes, my only coherent thought was for this ordeal to be over. As I lay there, I closed my eyes and focused on surviving the next few minutes. For some reason, I had convinced myself that this test would be the death of me.

Suddenly, my mind cleared, and my body seemed different—weightless, almost. I stood on the most beautiful beach my eyes have ever beheld. It was different from anything of which Earth boasts. I was transported in spirit to a new body and to another place—another dimension perhaps—somewhere beyond my imagination.

My eyes beheld never-before-seen colors, each one richer, bolder, and more vibrant than anything I knew existed. My vision became perfect without my glasses. In fact, my eyes detected details I did not think were possible for things both close and far away.

When I looked down, sand sparkled beneath my bare feet as I wiggled my toes in excitement. I picked up a handful of golden flecks that shimmered in the light, as if they were twinkling stars.

I also noticed that my body had become slim and healthy in every way. I seemed younger and more beautiful, and every part of me seemed to work in perfect harmony. An assessment of this new body revealed no aches or pains anywhere.

A light surrounded me and enveloped my entire being. A beautiful pure light, brighter yet less piercing than the sun. It moved around everything, bringing a sense of comfort and peace as if it were a gentle river flowing over every object. The air itself seemed to be alive.

I lifted my eyes. I turned my gaze to the ocean of crystal-clear water. It sparkled like diamonds on the surface, the water particles dancing in the pure joy of existence in the presence of the light.

I stood in awe of my surroundings. I turned to my right and beheld a golden beach going on and on for miles. As far as I could see, it did not end. Throughout the span, trees were scattered here and there. Some resembled palm trees, yet they had a unique look different from any I had seen on Earth or perhaps my new vision allowed me to experience details beyond my usual perception.

I then turned to the left to view more of the same endless beach. As I paused and looked up, I realized no sky existed—no clouds anywhere in the distance. Only a pure light encircled everything and seemed to move as if giving every element a gentle hug.

Strangely, I heard no sounds, only silence. Not even the water made noise as it gently caressed the beach in front of me. A peaceful quiet. Stillness. Time itself stood still. It did not even exist. I could stand on that spot for eternity and be content.

My imagination could not conjure up a more perfect place as I stood admiring everything in front of me.

Then, I felt the presence of my Lord and Savior.

Nothing else mattered. I let the sand in my hands trickle between my fingers and return to its home below.

When we think of Jesus, we can think of peace, but for me, the sensation went beyond peace. Nothing mattered except being in His presence. Everything became perfect.

Joy and exhilaration overcame me as if I were a small child experiencing the wonder and beauty of the world for the first time. Yet, nothing else mattered: no person, no place, no sensation—I became *complete* when in His presence.

I did not matter—not my body, not the pain I experienced, not my sorrow, not my tears, but joy beyond happiness. Beyond the moment, radiated an eternal joy. The raging battle ended within me. My desire became to stand still and soak in everything Jesus offered me.

At the same time, I felt like the most important person in all the universe. Jesus would come and spend a moment alone with me.

He approached from behind me. I did not move or turn. I would not leave. I waited. I waited on the

Lord. As He stepped directly behind me, He placed His hand on my right shoulder. A strange and beautiful sensation rushed through my entire body—electrifying, energizing, and uplifting, all in one. My body changed in an instance.

I breathed deeply, closing my eyes to soak in the moment and reopening them to the old world and body I had left behind.

A warm breeze brushed over me from head to toe, but the fan in the testing room no longer worked and this breeze came from the opposite direction. The warm air gave me a final hug before disappearing.

In fact, the testing room appeared pitch black. Silence and confusion greeted me. I lay there not yet comprehending the experience as the awe and wonder still rushed through me. I wanted to return to His presence and not be stuck in a non-working MRI machine.

God sent me back to the "old" me. Yet, I was different — changed forever. I wanted to get up and run back to that wonderful place, to turn and gaze upon His face, to never leave. However, I didn't know the way.

He had other plans, and I would have to wait a while longer to see Him in that form again.

Moments later, the technician walked through the door, fussing under his breath, or perhaps it was the foam stuffed in my ears.

Muttering, he explained as he pulled me and the table toward him, "This room is the only one in the hospital that lost power. I don't know what happened, but I don't want you to worry. Your test saved. In fact, I saw the brain tumor on the screen. It is still relatively small. Maybe they won't even have to do surgery if it doesn't grow and you don't have symptoms."

The tech had a softer tone in his voice this time, but he was still wanting to get the job done. I realized only the emergency lights were on, but they gave the tech enough light to work. He started preparing the IV. He remained both focused and frustrated. The time came to do the second set of tests involving contrast or a type of dye so the machine could pick up different details.

Seeing my confused look, he continued, "They are getting the power back up as we speak. I won't be able to see your second set of tests right now, but they will save for later review. The computer that saves the tests didn't lose power, just the machine and the rest of this room. So, don't worry. You won't have to come back and do this again and your doctor will call you with the results and a plan."

Thank you, Lord. I don't think I could go through this test again unless you promised to keep me with you.

As the fluid pumped through my veins, I suffered an anaphylactic reaction. I learned the sensation of drowning as I gasped for air.

"Oh, no! You would be the one in twenty-five thousand statistic," he said with a chuckle as he undid my head restraint and let me sit up. "Especially since I told you your chance of an allergic reaction to this was highly unlikely." He tried to keep me calm and cheerful through this ordeal as he had already witnessed the panicked look on my face.

His quick glances to his watch added to my anxiety.

I still gasped for air and did not respond other than to offer him a half smile as my breath returned slightly. Getting behind so early in the day would cause him and others to have an unusually long day. Therefore, he laid me, still struggling to breathe normally, back down and strapped me in again. He assured me I would be fine once my body absorbed all the dye.

The other lights came on and the machine started again. This time the close confines did not bother me. The noise became of no consequence. I lay there thinking of the experience God gave me, replaying it in my mind again and again.

I did not know what it all meant, but I longed to go back there. I knew without a doubt I did not want to be in this room and doing this test again. However, the second set seemed to go faster as my mind cleared, and my panic disappeared.

A few minutes later, as I left the room, I turned to tell the technician thank you, realizing I didn't even know his name. However, I was too late, he had already moved on to his next task. I greeted Robert sitting in the waiting area with bloodshot eyes giving away the fact that he had cried while I underwent the test.

"Ready to go?" he asked.

I nodded, and he wrapped his arm around me as we walked to the vehicle. This time, my steps were quicker. Life, not death, seemed to be ahead of my now.

"I prayed for you while you were in there. The need to pray overwhelmed me. While I prayed, I wrote out our kid's full names on a paper and as soon as I finished, a peaceful sensation came over me. I knew everything was going to be okay," He smiled at me and I returned the smile. "How did the test go?" He asked as he handed me the piece of paper.

John Robert Alexander Dyer

Savannah Rose Marie Dyer

Samantha Roxanne Marie Dyer

Sharon Rebekka Marie Dyer

Matthew Joseph Oliver Dyer

Mark Anthony Christian Dyer

Tranquility filled me, too, while I looked at their names and held it close to my heart.

After we made it to the vehicle, I answered

Robert's question: "I will tell you more about everything later. My chest is killing me. I had an allergic reaction to the dye they used for the second set of tests. I struggled to breathe so hard. Now, all of my ribs ache." I was still digesting the experience God granted me and was not yet ready to share it with others.

"I'll take you straight home then," he said and off we drove down the curving roads, up and down hills, until we reached our driveway.

Robert helped me into our home. Our kids ran to embrace me as I walked in the door. I soaked up every bit of their love and thanked God for more moments like these.

I lay down on the couch. My thoughts were still processing the events that had happened. I did not understand. Only a desire to be wholly in the Lord's presence and never leave it remained. I did not understand why God sent me back, but I was so thankful He took me on the journey.

Later in the evening, Robert came into the house to check on me, asking, "How are you feeling now?"

I replied, "My chest is still killing me from

gasping for breath so hard, but my head hasn't hurt at all." As if I had won a major victory, the warriors retreated into hiding. However, I only expected the respite to be temporary. For months, they had only been temporary.

I also realized my thinking remained clearer than…well, ever. No searing pains or attacks affected me for the entire rest of the day. I was able to move through a doorway without running into a wall when I walked to the bathroom. Amazing! But what did it all mean?

I asked Robert to sit beside me, and I recounted the entire sequence of events to him, trying not to leave out any of the details. We realized we had both experienced a spiritual moment with God that day. I was in awe realizing how God was with us both at the same time in unique and beautiful ways.

CONFIRMATION

This is the day which the LORD hath made;
we will rejoice and be glad in it.
Psalm 118:24

The following day my headaches were still gone. My thoughts were even clearer. I got up in the morning and started working early. I got more accomplished in a few hours before lunch than I had managed in all the months combined the entire year.

In addition, the calls, emails, and even written letters of prayer continued to come in steadily. I cherished each one of them.

I walked into the kitchen to fix lunch with a smile on my face and a skip in my step.

"You must be feeling better today, Mom," John stated with joy on his face.

"I am," I replied. "I am better today than I have been all year long." Even better than the last several years, I thought to myself.

"What do you all want for lunch? I will cook today," I told them all, confident in my ability to handle this task for a change.

Once lunch ended, I went back into my office. I continued to catch up on what seemed to be a mountain of tasks that had piled up during the past few months. Each one mostly small, but finally getting my attention.

I even fixed Sam's computer, and Robert prepared to deliver it to him in the afternoon. This time I would not have to go with Robert because the repair only involved replacement of a fan and needed no explanation. I kept working in my office until late in the afternoon.

Reeda Faye called to check up on me. "How did the test go?" she asked.

I answered, "I don't understand what happened to me yesterday, but I experienced something amazing, and my relationship with God is closer than in all of my life."

"That's wonderful," Reeda Faye replied. "And you're still better today?"

"Yes, I'm better than I have been for a long time, longer than I can remember," I answered.

"Elizabeth, I think God healed you," she said with authority.

"I am uncertain about what happened," I stated, "but I admit it was out of this world." The possibility of a healing did not occur to me before.

We were still talking when I received a call on the other line. "Reeda Faye, it's the doctor's office calling. Can you hold on while I take their call?"

"Yes, I'll hold. Grab it quickly," she replied.

"Hello," I stated after I clicked the flash button on the phone.

"Hello, is this Elizabeth?" the nurse on the phone asked.

"Yes, this is Elizabeth," I stated with bated breath. I knew that hearing from a instead of the doctor, usually signaled at least better news.

"I just called to let you know we received your MRI results back and everything's normal," she stated matter-of-factly.

"What?" I asked.

"Yes, your results came in, and everything is normal. Were you hoping something would be wrong?" she said with a chuckle, joking with me.

"No," I started laughing. "But just a few days ago I found out I had a brain tumor, but if the results are now normal, that means God did, in fact, heal me."

"Well, when they did the test with the contrast, it showed everything to be normal. No tumor present," she stated, repeating the diagnosis.

"This is just wonderful news! Thank you so much for calling," I said, almost yelling from the excitement.

"I'm glad I could give you good news," she stated as we ended the conversation.

I clicked the button to get back to Reeda Faye. "Reeda Faye," I shouted, "It's gone! It's really and truly gone!"

"Praise the Lord," she said. "Praise the Lord."

"I have to run tell all my family. Thank you so much for all your love and prayers," I told her.

"All the glory goes to God," she said as we hung up.

With the phone call, I finally understood. God took my death sentence and gave me a new life. When the doctor's office called with normal test results, I accepted that God had healed me. I became the recipient of a miracle!

Jesus won the war and shared the spoils of victory with me, His unworthy servant.

What was next? A journey.

A journey that proved to be like none I have ever experienced before. God molding me and shaping me into a new person, the person God wanted me to be as His follower.

Now, I became ready for whatever God brought my way. Anticipating, basking in joy, and almost giddy, I looked forward to what awaits around the bend. Now, I can face death with joy, knowing what comes next.

Elizabeth Dyer

EPILOGUE
JOY & GUILT

...weeping may endure for a night,
but joy cometh in the morning.
Psalm 30:5b

My healing had come on August 27, 2009. In the days, weeks, and months after, God started restoring my health, not to the sensation of the new body I experienced, but closer than I had experienced on Earth. Little by little, I even started losing weight. I also started a new practice: laughing. Laughter became a regular sound in my home.

A merry heart doeth good like a medicine: but a broken spirit drieth the bones. Proverbs 17:22.

I stopped worrying about all the tasks at hand and began enjoying the moment in which I lived. I realized, again, just how short life can be, and I understood God wanted me to be joyful. He wanted joy in my heart even when circumstances kept me from being happy. Spreading joy should be one of the missions of every Christian.

Previously, I had sought after happiness—the American Dream. I worked trying to earn the things I believed I deserved. I put in long hours, pushing myself to the limit and beyond.

However, joy and happiness are not the same. I had confused them too many times. I had sought happiness, which meant things should be going my way. Everything I desired should be mine, not just everything I needed.

Now the God of hope fill you with all joy and peace in believing, that ye may abound in hope, through the power of the Holy Ghost. Romans 15:13.

Joy, on the other hand, meant learning contentment, loving what God had provided, loving when my needs were met and even when my wants were put aside.

Joy meant appreciation for the sacrifice Jesus had made for me—yes, even for me. Jesus loved me more than I deserved and beyond anything I could earn. Pure joy in this realization let me see others in a new light. It allowed me to love others without the fear of not being loved in return.

It let me see how we are all on the same level— searching for unconditional love, living in our sin, and needing a Savior. I found joy in being able to share my Savior with others. I found joy in fellowship with His children and joy in loving others who viewed themselves as unlovable. Yes, I found joy in loving those who were just like me and those who were completely different as well.

For all have sinned, and come short of the glory of God Romans 3:23.

I knew I remained unworthy of the miracle God had given me. I considered myself unworthy even with the spirit of rejection gone. Yet, God blessed me beyond measure. I cannot tell you why God healed me while others died. However, I am certain I no longer want to waste the time God has given me.

I search for His purpose for my days; I seek His direction. I face my fears with Him at my side. I know now I am loved in a way I could never understand. I believe all things are possible through Christ and now I live it! I pray for you to find this truth for yourself.

I can do all things through Christ which strengtheneth me. Philippians 4:13.

With my health restored, I returned to work full time from home. However, during the time following my healing and even now, we struggle financially. Once an individual gets so far behind on the bills, it is difficult to catch up. I am working the debt snowball and following Dave Ramsey's financial advise, but the road ahead is long.

We must keep our faith and realize God will provide and bless our work. I hope to one day see past baby step two. I am still praying for a miracle in this area of my life, now that I understand miracles are not in such short supply. *(See DaveRamsey.com for all of the baby steps)*

Notwithstanding, lest we should offend them, go thou to the sea, and cast an hook, and take up the fish that first cometh up; and when thou hast opened his mouth, thou shalt find a piece of money: that take, and give unto them for me and thee. Matthew 17:27.

The most unexpected phenomena became the ongoing connection with others experiencing tumors, cancer, and especially brain cancer. God sent many my way through the health food store and smoothie bar. I opened it in my quest to help others achieve optimal health as well—S&S Smoothies and Supplements in Blairsville.

I have prayed for hundreds of individuals suffering much the same way I did for all of those months. Some are completely healed, some have gone on to be with Jesus, and some are still fighting the battles cancer creates.

However, none touched my heart as much as six-year-old Caleb Kinnersley. When his parents, Kevin and Janna, plus his sister, Anna Beth, got the news of his brain tumor in August 2011. They asked others to join them in prayer.

I went to school with Kevin and became deeply saddened when I heard the news about his son. As a parent, I appreciate just how much we long to take any pain away from our children.

I felt an unmistakable connection to young Caleb not only because of his condition, but because we also shared a November birthday. My healing had come in August two years before, and I prayed for God to give the same miracle to Caleb this August.

God, this child is too young to go through

everything I experienced. Lord, Please spare him from the pain. Lord, you worked a miracle for me, PLEASE give one to young Caleb, too.

I became part of the Facebook group—Team Caleb—and prayed for this young warrior every day. We kept informed of his worsening condition. By early November, he could no longer sit up on his own. The treatments were affecting the cancer, but his body grew weaker.

God, you healed me two years ago. I lived two years more than I ever expected. Caleb is only six, Lord. I will switch places with him if You will allow me to, oh Lord.

My life has been full and I know what awaits me on the other side. Lord, take me to be with You and let this young child grow up to be a man. Lord, there is nothing else I can offer as a sacrifice, but myself.

I had witnessed the same thing with my dad for months in the hospital. Cancer is evil. Sin brought it into the world, and it attacks the righteous and unrighteous alike. It knows no boundaries. As its tentacles grow and spread, it mutates cells everywhere it touches.

It does not cease until it destroys the host that keeps it alive. Yes, I recognized the ugly face of cancer and rejoice to think of the day it will be destroyed forever, the day no one will again experience this wretched disease.

God did not take me instead of Caleb, and he gave up the fight on December 12, 2011. I still mourn for the loss of that little boy, for the pain his parents go through every day, and for the hole left in their hearts and in their families. I cannot write this without crying for them.

The Kinnersleys still mourn for Caleb. His memory will live forever in their hearts as his spirit will live forever with God. Caleb is only gone from Earth, but not really gone at all.

After his passing, I became angry at God again.

Why did you take him, Lord? Why couldn't you take me instead? His family is heartbroken. The community is heartbroken. He was too young to die.

God could handle my anger and through it He revealed something I was not expecting. He revealed my guilt at still being alive and a jealousy inside me I had not seen.

I became jealous of Caleb. I realized where he was. I experienced only a fraction of what he got to behold now. God did not let me pass the beautiful beaches. However, from the Scripture, I perceive there are cities with streets of gold, mansions, angels, cherubim, and things I cannot even imagine.

And the twelve gates were twelve pearls: every several gate was of one pearl: and the street of the city was pure gold, as it were transparent glass. Revelation 21:21.

I am also certain Caleb found the most beautiful ski slopes to enjoy. I bet he is setting records racing down them right now.

And most importantly, I sense he is in the presence of Jesus. He has no pain and no sorrow. He has a new body just like I got to experience, and he isn't even missing anyone. For when his family joins him, it will seem as if no time has passed for him. As if he just turned around and there they were. Oh, what a joyful reunion it will be!

And though I never got to meet Caleb here on Earth, I will see him one day and take my family to introduce them. The joy of the Lord will sustain us both here now and forever in Heaven. May God give you peace through all the trials you must face.

My brethren, count it all joy when ye fall into divers temptations; Knowing this, that the trying of your faith worketh patience. James 1:2-3.

My prayer is for you to develop a relationship with the Lord and experience joy all the days of your life!

Elizabeth Dyer

GOD'S PLAN OF SALVATION
BY REVEREND TODD FLANAGAN

*For God so loved the world, that he gave his only
begotten Son, that whosoever believeth in him should not
perish, but have everlasting life.*
John 3:16

From the time Adam and Eve were evicted from the Garden of Eden, mankind has fallen short of the ideals God has placed before them. We call these shortcomings sin. Sin separates us from the perfect will of God. Isaiah 59:2 says, "*But your iniquities have separated you and your God, and your sins have hid His face from you, that He will not hear.*"

However, to correct the situation, Jesus Christ provides the perfect and only remedy. John 14:6 says, "*Jesus saith unto Him, I am the way, the truth, and the life: no man cometh unto the Father, but by me.*"

Christ died for the sins of all mankind, thus making Him the ultimate sacrifice. We are promised in John 3:16 *"that whosoever believeth in Him should not perish, but have everlasting life."* So, how does one receive Christ? We all reach a point in our lives where we realize we are lost. We know we are without hope and we are devoid of God's love. When we are in this condition, we are told in Romans 10:13 *"For whosoever shall call upon the name of the Lord shall be saved."* The lost soul must come before God, expressing faith in Jesus Christ as their Savior and asking forgiveness of their sins.

In order for a person to be saved, they must:

Recognize they are lost.

Understand Jesus Christ died for them as the ultimate atonement for their sins.

Pray to God, acknowledging faith in Christ, and asking forgiveness of their sins.

Once you accept Christ as your personal Savior, it is only the beginning of a greater work He has planned for you. It is important to involve yourself in a church with other believers of Christ to further your relationship and increase your knowledge and understanding of God's word.

PHOTO ALBUM

The memory of the just is blessed...
Proverbs 10:7

MARCH 2009

John and Matthew's Birthday Party

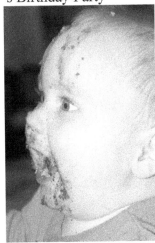

John with his card

Matthew Enjoying Cake

Savannah

Sharon

Granny Irene's Funeral

Robert with Our "Cooperative" Kids

Samantha

Savannah

John

Sharon

Vietta Mae—Back Row, Center
with Her Brother's and Sisters

APRIL 2009

Sharon

Matthew

Our Aquarium & Homeschool Project

MAY 2009

Airshow—Dobbins Air Force Base

Savannah Smiling for the Camera As Always

Japanese Val Replica

John Actually Getting Tired at the End of the Day

SBD Dauntless

Matthew—Our Escape Artist

C17

Outing for a Belated Mother's Day Celebration

Samantha Unaware I had the Camera

Savannah and Sharon Posing

Doing My Best to Get Them All Looking the Right Way at The Greenville Zoo, Sc

Robert and Sharon watching the Giraffe

*John Being His
Adventurous Self*

*Matthew Fascinated with
Baby Bob*

Elizabeth Dyer

At The South Carolina Botanical Gardens—Clemson, SC

Matthew Enjoying Some Freedom in the Grassy Field

Miss Savannah Always Ready for a Picture

Sharon After Rolling in the Grass

Samantha Putting on a Show

JUNE 2009

Birthday Party—Mayors Park—Young Harris, GA

Proud Dad

Savannah Being a Dinosaur

John on the Chase

Sharon Being a Stegosauraus

Samantha Enjoing the Swings

A Rare Photo Which Includes Me

Mark's Arrival

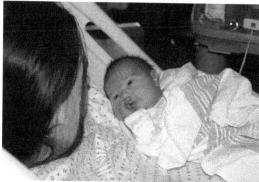

Holding Mark for the First time

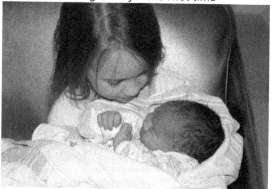

Savannah Fasinated by Her Baby Brother

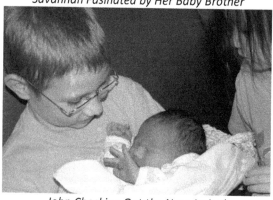

John Checking Out the New Arrival

Samantha Not Sure What to Think

Matthew Just Having Fun

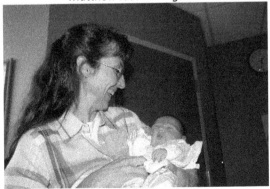

Miss Sheila

JULY 2009

4th of July

Almost All looking at the Camera

John on Another Adventure

Savannah Barefoot as Always

A Moment to Relax

No Time to Stop and Eat

Watchful Dad

Fly-in—Gainesville, GA

Our Plane Enthusiasts

John Loving the Planes

One Taking Off Caught Someone's Attention

Sharon's Birthday Party—Vogel State Park, Blairsville, GA

The Birthday Girl—All Smiles

Stopping Long Enough for a Photo

Different Playground— Different Equipment

Bare Feet on Grass

The World is Brand New

Climbing to the Top

ABOUT THE AUTHOR

*O magnify the Lord with me, and let us
exalt his name together.*
Psalm 34:3

Elizabeth Dyer lived this story, and God has led her to tell it. To boast upon the Lord and all He had done for her. These pages alone do not contain a fraction of all the wonderful things God has brought into her life. She prays for you to have a close and personal relationship with your creator, your savior, the one true God.

Elizabeth lives in Blairsville, Georgia with her husband and their six children.

Elizabeth Dyer is an entrepreneur, author, and speaker. She owns more than five businesses including a health food store. Elizabeth's mission in life is to help others live their best life possible, by looking at the body, mind, and spirit as one.

Elizabeth derives inspiration from her six children, friends, and clients. She utilizes both struggles and triumphs to help others, showing that blessings come not only when we are on the mountaintop, but through heartaches in the valleys as well. Be sure to connect through ElizabethDyer.Me to keep up with her latest adventures.

If you would like to book Elizabeth to speak at a conference or your church, contact her at admin@elizabethdyer.me.

DID THIS BOOK HELP YOU?

Rejoicing in hope; patient in tribulation; continuing instant in prayer;
Romans 12:12

Did this book help you in any way? If so, please consider sharing your experience by leaving a 5-Star review on any of your favorite bookstores' website so others may also find hope in these chapters.

Thank you and God Bless.

Printed in the USA
CPSIA information can be obtained
at www.ICGtesting.com
CBHW051557171024
15995CB00014B/1088